The Thriving Woman's Guide to Setting Boundaries

Kim Buck, M.B.A.

The Thriving Woman's Guide to Setting Boundaries
Kim Buck, M.B.A.

Published by The Catalyst Group International Inc.
Calgary, Alberta T2W 0M2 Canada
403-255-3235

Copyright © 2015 by Kim Buck
First Edition, 2015

Published in Canada

ISBN: 978-0-9739939-7-4

TABLE of CONTENTS

About the Author
Dedication
Acknowledgement
Disclaimer

About the Author

 **Kim Buck, M.B.A.,** an Empowerment Coach and catalyst, is the founder of Are You Willing to Be Seen? Coaching and the author of *The Thriving Woman's Guide to*™ series. She helps women release what is holding them back from living the life they desire.
For information see www.areyouwillingtobeseen.com.

DEDICATION

I dedicate this book to Kayla, Coda and Sadie. It was through them, in part, that I started seeking out information that is contained in this book. Kayla, you showed me what pure joy looks like. When I think of joy, I think of you. Coda, you showed me what living in your purpose looks like. I will try to live in my purpose the way you simply were your purpose. Sadie, you showed me what true resilience looks like. You had the capacity to be happy in spite of the hardships you endured.

ACKNOWLEDGEMENT

I would like to thank the amazing women who shared their stories with me. All of these stories are real but all of the names have been changed. The information in this book comes from my interactions with many wonderful people. The people who have had the greatest impact on me are included here. As well, I received support and encouragement for this book from people I cherish. I would like to express my gratitude and appreciation to:

Crystal Andrus, a trailblazer whose concepts of Mother Energy™, Daughter Energy™ and Woman Energy™ showed up for me at a time when I really needed them.

Wendy Buck, my beautifully intuitive sister, who helped me stay the course when I felt like I had information overload.

Ellie Drake, a delicious mentor who taught me how to live in a parasympathetic state of ease.

Mark Giovanetto, my wonderful husband, who stands tall in Man Energy™ and desires the best for me.

Tara Marino, a beautiful mentor who lives her life awake and fully engaged and who expresses beauty and truth with elegance.

Colleen Pilling, a wonderful, wise mentor who taught me the difference between concession and compromise and instilled in me the belief that I had the right to set boundaries.

DISCLAIMER

This book is designed to provide information on how to set boundaries in different areas of your life. It is sold with the understanding that the publisher and author are not engaged in rendering legal or other professional services. If legal or other expert assistance is required, the services of a competent professional should be sought.

It is not the purpose of this manual to reprint all the information that is otherwise available to women who desire to set boundaries, but instead to complement, amplify and supplement other texts. You are urged to read all the available material, learn as much as possible about setting boundaries and tailor the information to your individual needs.

Setting boundaries is an individual process and no one process is the best way for all individuals. Every effort has been made to make this manual as complete and accurate as possible. However, there may be mistakes, both typographical and in content. Therefore, this text should be used only as a general guide and not as the ultimate source of boundary setting.

The purpose of this manual is to educate and entertain. The author and The Catalyst Group International Inc. shall have neither liability nor responsibility to any person or entity with respect to any loss or damage caused, or alleged to have been caused, directly or indirectly, by the information contained in this book.

If you do not wish to be bound by the above, you may return this book to the publisher for a full refund.

INTRODUCTION

My Story

Until a few years ago, I could have been the poster woman for "this woman desperately needs boundaries." Until that point, I didn't really have any boundaries or any idea what boundaries looked like. All I knew was that other women didn't seem to be burned out like I was. I was full of anger, resentment and exhaustion. Somehow over time, I became the person in my family who took care of everyone and I carried everyone, in one way or another.

I grew up with a rage-aholic mother. My two sisters and I never knew what would set mom off or when the explosive rage would happen. When my mom was in one of her fits of rage, she could be quite violent. One day, when I was about 6 or 7 years old, my mom bashed my sisters' heads and my head into a wall, because in her words, "she was knocking some sense into us." We were fortunate that she didn't knock our basic functioning out of us. These rage episodes instilled in me the belief that I was responsible for my mom's happiness and I felt compelled to do whatever it took to make her happy. It didn't matter what I was required to do as long as it made my mom happy. I had no boundaries. My sisters and I weren't allowed to have boundaries. My mom didn't have any boundaries either. We weren't allowed to express anger. My mom felt that she was the only one who was entitled to be angry. So she expressed it frequently all the while feeling like she was the victim. She would yell and bang doors and throw things. It was terrifying. My mom was well-controlled in public, though. Generally, no one outside of our house knew that mom had a violent temper that could go off at any time for any reason. I once heard Dr. Northrup, a leading expert on women's health, say that if your mother was angry when she was pregnant with you, you will feel compelled to make her happy as you grow up. I believe that to be true.

My mother was a master rescuer. She was always the hero in a crisis so much so that she became addicted to solving crises and often created crises in order solve them and be the hero. My mom had low self-esteem and being the hero in a crisis helped her feel better about herself. This feeling lasted a very short time and then she would need a new crisis to resolve.

My maternal grandmother had cancer for a lot of my mom's life. My mom provided most of the care for her mom. My grandmother passed away when my mom was around 26. My mom's only sister didn't do much and wasn't much of a support. My grandfather spent most of his time and money with other women. My mom was in Mother Energy™ - Taken Advantage of with her mom and sister and she was in Mother Energy™ - Intrusive with everyone else in her life, with the exception of me. For whatever reason, my mom was in Daughter Energy™ (and both sides of it) with me. This required me to be in Mother Energy™ - Taken Advantage of with her. These terms are explained in this book.

From quite an early age, my mom treated me like I was her confidante. She burdened me with her problems, but thankfully not all of them. She talked about her and my dad's financial problems, her issues at work, etc.. I didn't have the psychological development as a child to understand these issues. All of this information just made my world feel unsafe. It didn't matter. Of course I couldn't solve these problems but I did feel they were mine to figure out.

When I was 19, my mom had a massive heart attack. When she came home from the hospital, it took her a year to get back on her feet. I took care of her during this time. I lived at home so it was "convenient" that I take care of her. I was in my first year of university at the time. I was overwhelmed with the demands of my course load and providing care for my mom. No one else, including my dad, provided care to mom, so I just continued to do it. I wanted my mom to be well so I was willing to do whatever it took to get her well. My family members – my dad, my two sisters and my mom's sister, who lived with us, all wanted mom well but they thought it was "best" if I provided all of the care. This way, none of them had to do it. They all had "important, time-consuming things" that required their time, energy and focus. It wasn't like I had nothing going on in my life. It was just that no one thought my needs, time or energy mattered because I didn't know that I had the right to state that they did. I did whatever it took to get my mom well.

I wanted her to be well. My mom wanted to be "well enough". There is a big difference between being well and being well enough. A big part of my mom understood very clearly that being well enough meant that she could get back to her life but she would always be on my mind and I would always be putting energy into her by way of wondering, "Is she okay? Will she get sick again?" If mom was well, I would have been able to get back to my life fully. Being well enough kept her in the top of my mind and kept me tied to her.

This was very manipulative behavior on my mom's part. It took me 20 years to understand that I couldn't want my mom to be well more than she wanted to be well. It didn't matter how much care I provided, mom was going to be well to the level that worked for her. This is a really critical point for women to understand – you can't want more for someone than they want for themselves. You will only burn yourself out trying to get this person to your desired level of whatever it is you desire for them – wellness, income, stability, dreams, etc. If you get nothing else from this book but the understanding that you can't want "it" more for them than they want it for themselves, then this book has served you.

I erroneously believed that if I did more for my mom, she would be well. As an example, if mom had a dinner party, I would go over after it was done to clean up so that she wouldn't exhaust herself. It didn't matter that I was exhausted. It was just important that she wasn't exhausted. I totally understand now that if my mom felt it was important for her to have a dinner party and she felt that she had the energy for that, then she had the energy to clean up after it as well. Or, she needed to find a different way to clean up – hire it out, get my dad to do it, whatever.

A year and a half later, my husband, then fiancé, was in a serious motor vehicle accident. He was hospitalized for a month and required a lot of care after that. Even though he lived at home at the time (he was in university), everyone at his house expected me to look after him. I didn't want to let my husband down so I provided all of the care. This was grueling, demanding and exhausting. I had just finished looking after my mom and now I was looking after my fiancé. I ended up with Chronic Fatigue Syndrome about six months after my husband recovered. I lost a year of university because of the Chronic Fatigue and it took me almost six years to finally be well from it.

Three and a half years after my husband's accident, my mom had cancer. Even though I wasn't fully well and was back at university part-time, I provided all of the care for my mom. It was convenient for everyone but me for me to do all of the heavy work.

My mom would go on to have another heart attack six years later. I was married by this point but I still felt that it was my duty to look after my mom. It was harder now because I was working full-time. I would go over to mom's house every night after work and do whatever she needed. My dad wasn't required to do anything and quite likely he wouldn't have done anything anyways. My dad operated from Son

Energy™ and would fluctuate between The Son and Indifferent depending on the situation.

My mom and dad were involved in a serious highway motor vehicle accident six years later. Both of them were significantly injured but in different ways. My dad suffered a heart attack during the accident and required by-pass surgery a few months later. My mom suffered significant soft tissue damage, a broken hand and a brain injury. Fortunately for my parents and unfortunately for me, I had lost my job 10 days before their accident so I was "conveniently" available to look after both of them. This was beyond grueling and I was beyond overwhelmed. I didn't know whether I was coming or going and I was running on fumes. It took me two years to recover from this heavy load.

My mom passed away three and a half years after the accident. By the time she passed away, I was completely empty. I was relieved because at least this big, draining part of my life had come to completion. Unfortunately for me, because I still didn't have any boundaries and I had no sense of having the right to say NO I simply got sucked into the endless pit of my family's crises after my mom died. My oldest sister's marriage was falling apart and she was suicidal. My middle sister was scheduled for surgery and required assistance afterward. My father was having panic attacks at night. I took care of all of this. I was festering with anger and hostility. I was full of grief from my mom's passing but I didn't have any time or space to grieve. I had no time for my own life. It was simply go, go, go and go faster and go some more. I gave and gave and gave until I had no more to give and then I gave more. I got stuck finding assisted living arrangements for my aunt. I got stuck organizing home care for my father. I listened endlessly to my oldest sister go on about how her life was falling apart.

By the end of the year, my father made the decision to move into a senior's residence. This meant that the house that I grew up in and in which my parents lived for 38 years, needed to be emptied and renovated so that it could be sold. Since I was the person who always did everything, which allowed everyone else to do nothing, I got stuck emptying out 38 years of stuff. This was a big job and I was the only one doing it. I had no boundaries with my father or with my sisters. Everyone simply expected me to do it because it had always been that way. I emptied out the house and my husband organized the renos. We had the house ready for sale by April of that year. Because being responsible for selling his own house was too much for my father, I was in charge of that as well.

Since my mom's passing, I have had a few key turning point moments that helped me set boundaries. The first came in June of that year. The house hadn't sold yet and I was desperate to get my life back. A friend of mine is a medium. I had a channeled session with my mom. She very clearly gave me the permission I required to hand over everything to my father to let him deal with everything that was his to deal with. My mom also very clearly told me that all of this endless work on behalf of others was killing me. It hadn't occurred to me until that point in time that this crappy, endless, exhausting, thankless work was killing me. Enough said. I handed everything back to my father and told him that he was required to be responsible for himself.

After my mom died, I got stuck with my aunt's care. She had had a stroke before my mom passed away and another one nine months later. Having no boundaries for myself, I got stuck making arrangements for assisted living for my aunt, being named as her Enduring Power of Attorney, taking her to all of her medical appointments, receiving all of the calls from the hospital when she was admitted over and over for this and that, dealing with the attitudes of the care providers and on and on. It wasn't until I had a conversation with the social worker, assigned to my aunt's file, that I finally stopped doing all of this. This was turning point number two. The social worker told me that I wasn't a bad person for not wanting to do all of this work on my aunt's behalf. She said that it would be okay if I allowed "the system" to take care of my aunt. This was the permission I required to stop doing all of this for my aunt.

The social worker had a grandmother who was an alcoholic for most of her adult life. This social worker understood that selfish people don't get to demand our time, energy and resources just because they are family members. The grandmother of the social worker was in a nursing home at the time of our conversation. The social worker said that no one in her family visited the grandmother and the staff at the nursing home thought the family members were horrible people for not having respect for their elderly family member. The social worker told me the reason no one in the family visited the grandmother was because the grandmother was a selfish, thoughtless person who had no interest in the social worker's mom growing up or in her granddaughter, the social worker, when she was growing up. The social worker said that her grandmother didn't get to demand attention just because she was old and sick. She said that even though the staff at the home had lots of judgment around the family's absence, the family stood firm on the belief that this woman did not deserve the family's time, energy and attention. The family chose to have a strong boundary around this and honor themselves. This conversation was liberating for me and it gave me the permission I needed to have boundaries with my aunt. I am giving you permission to have the boundaries you require with selfish, demanding family members and friends and to honor yourself. If you are one of those selfish, demanding family members, know that people are not at your beck and call. It is not selfish of your friends or family members to say no regardless of how dependent you may be on them. It is time for you to find your own way.

My aunt has been in a nursing home for almost five years now. I didn't help her move in and I haven't seen her once. I haven't been to any of the medical consultations with her medical team. I didn't take her phone calls when she first moved in. The only thing I have done for my aunt over this time is to make sure her bills are paid. I still have Enduring Power of Attorney for her which requires me to ensure her financial affairs are up to date.

The nursing home wasn't well equipped to handle my aunt's move from assisted care to nursing care because they expect the family to do it. Unfortunately, "the system" acts like a Daughter Energy™

– Entitled woman and demands that family members do the hard lifting. I understand that "the system" is short of funds and that everyone working in it is overworked and underpaid. However, that is not my problem and I am not here on earth to take care of the needs of a selfish, greedy woman who only cares about herself. My aunt is undeserving of my time and energy and I have other things that I need to put those towards.

The third turning point regarding setting boundaries happened for me a couple of years ago. I came across the information on Mother Energy™, Daughter Energy™ and Woman Energy™. The light bulb went off in my head. I had provided all of the care to my mom, father, aunt and sisters without any of them asking for this help. I simply jumped in and provided it because it seemed like no one else was going to do it. I didn't understand when my mom first got sick that if I didn't provide the care then someone else would have to. Perhaps it would have been my father. Perhaps my sisters would have figured out a way to do it. I also didn't understand that when my husband was in his accident, if I hadn't provided all of his care then someone in his family would have had to. Perhaps his mother would have been required to or his father or even his brother. The problem was, however, that once I started being the dependable person who always took care of everyone, then no one had to step up to do it. I gave everyone an easy way out. I didn't understand that I didn't have to say yes to everything every time. I get that now. I understand now that I have the right to say no to everything and all things and that in doing so, I honor myself and require others to step up.

I share my story with you because I want you to avoid going through the hell that I went through. When all of this started, I was young and didn't know better. I was expected to do what I did but that didn't mean that I had to do what I did. Being the dependable one is a slippery slope to a disengaged life where you are doing thankless work that everyone thinks is easy, because they aren't the ones doing it. Being the dependable one drains you of your life force, your dreams and any sense of sanity. My wish for you is that you understand from my story that your story doesn't have to go this way. If you are starting on this path, know to your core that you can say no. Know to your core that you have the right to set boundaries and live your life in a more peaceful, engaged way. Know to your core that you are not here, on earth, to save everyone. That is not your job. That is not your responsibility. Know to your core that you deserve to live your life and not carry others through theirs.

SECTION ONE

Understanding Boundaries and Why They are Required

1

What is a Boundary?

Before I started writing this book, I would mention to women that I was going to write a book on setting boundaries. Every woman I mentioned the book title to said the same thing. They all said that they needed to understand more about boundaries and that setting boundaries was a challenge for them.

Everyone talks about setting boundaries as though everyone understands what a boundary is, why you would "set" a boundary and what the outcome of setting boundaries is. Unfortunately, few people seem to understand exactly what a boundary is. I am guessing that you picked up this book because something wasn't working well in your life and you feel that setting boundaries will hopefully make your life run better.

Boundaries are actually multidimensional, meaning that they are made up of different aspects and characteristics. At its most basic level, we have physical boundaries that define our physical space. These are property lines and they let everyone know what property is yours and what property is mine. As a society, we fully support the idea and act of establishing boundaries around our physical space. We understand and fully accept that having a fence defining the property line of our house makes sense.

There is even an expression that says, "Strong fences make for good neighbors." It lets people know where our physical property starts and ends. As a society, we understand that there are defined consequences for crossing that property line. If you cross that line uninvited, you might be charged with trespassing or some other violation.

As a society, we understand and fully accept that your property is not my responsibility to take care of. We also understand and accept that my property is not your responsibility to take care of. As well, we understand and accept that you don't get to paint my fence any color you please just because you feel like it and I don't get to cut down your trees just because the leaves from these trees are bothersome to me. As well, I am not required to mow your lawn because you are too lazy to do it or you feel entitled that someone else should do it for you. We all understand that you don't get to walk into my house uninvited to sit down and watch TV and we all understand that I don't get to crawl through your window and clean your bedroom because it seems messy to me when I look into your window from my bedroom. All of these actions seem ridiculous and we fully understand and fully accept the boundaries that come with property lines and that there are consequences for violating them.

Where we, as a society, struggle however, is with understanding the depth of boundaries and why they are required for the other critical areas of our lives. We somehow know that there is more to boundaries than just property lines defining our physical space but very few people can actually articulate the full meaning of a boundary. Because we are more than just physical space, we need a definition for boundaries that speaks to all the parts of us. There is a strange and pervasive belief that setting boundaries around our physical energy, mental and emotional well-being and psychological, psychic and spiritual space is wrong and selfish yet it is in these areas that we must focus if we want to live a life that is fulfilling and joyful.

As much as we, as women, understand the concept of a property line defining our physical space and the consequences that come with violating that property line, we struggle to understand the consequences of not respecting someone's mental, emotional, psychological, psychic and spiritual spaces. Some women have no problem crawling into your personal affairs to fix your "mess" and some women have no trouble expecting me to do their project at work because they don't feel like it. Some women have no problem telling you it is selfish to drop something on your to-do list that they want you to take care of. Some women have no problem offering me advice on how to live my life even though I didn't ask. Some women have no problem telling you that you don't have the right to lighten your load. Some expect you to bail them out of their situation and not be bothered by it. You might be any or all of these women. When it comes to our physical energy, our mental and emotional well-being and our psychological, psychic and spiritual spaces, we think it is selfish, greedy, unkind or not nice to have limits in place that others have to respect and not violate.

A lot of women struggle with the question of whether they have the right to set boundaries. What if the boundary hurts someone's feelings? What if setting a boundary makes you seem like you aren't a kind, understanding or nice person? Boundaries really have nothing to do with being kind or understanding or a nice person. They are operating instructions for you and everyone you interact with. If you thought of boundaries as operating instructions for your "system" and everyone with whom you interacted had these instructions to follow, it wouldn't be so hard for you to establish boundaries. We have internal operating instructions for ourselves and we have external operating instructions for everything or everyone outside of ourselves.

Think of software for a moment. What would happen if you needed to interact with a particular software program, like Microsoft Word, and you had no instructions? Likely you would end up feeling quite frustrated by the experience and you would be feeling overwhelmed and possibly defeated as well. This is also true of human interactions. If your internal and external instructions are fuzzy, unclear or absent, your interactions with yourself and everyone in your life will be difficult, irritating, frustrating and challenging. The clearer you can be on how you want to treat yourself and be treated, what your needs are, what your dreams and desires are, and what your truth is, the easier it will be for you and other people to treat you that way. It will also be easier for your needs to be met, your desires and dreams to be fulfilled and for your truth to be heard. Dr. Philip McGraw of the Dr. Phil show always says, "You teach people how to treat you." These operating instructions are your teaching instructions. How do you want your spouse to treat you? What kind of household activities do you require your spouse to participate in? What are the rules for your children? What expectations do you have for them? How do you want them to treat you? How do you want other family members to treat you? Are you allowing everyone to treat you however they feel like? What are your limits on other people's expectations of you? What are you doing about meeting your needs? What are you doing about fulfilling your dreams and desires? Have you spoken your truth?

The really great thing about operating instructions is that on a subconscious level, everyone is seeking to uncover them. It is very unsettling for people to push for a limit and not come in contact with one. You see this quite easily with children. They push and push and push until they find a limit that causes them to snap back. If there is no limit, they keep pushing. They are searching for the boundary.

Boundaries, or the snap-back point, in terms of behavior, help people feel more at ease. People may not like your snap-back point but it brings them great psychological comfort knowing one is in place and how far they can push. Psychological boundaries let people know when they have crossed the line. What are the consequences for crossing that line? These consequences need to be defined in your operating instructions. That way everyone knows what will happen when your line is violated. You need to honor these and follow through with the consequence each time your line is violated. In doing so, you are honoring yourself and teaching people how to treat you.

Marianne is a manager with a team of 3 people directly reporting to her and up to 40 people who indirectly report to her. One of Marianne's direct reports, Sally, had a horribly painful childhood. Sally is now in her early thirties and she has yet to heal all of the trauma she experienced years ago. In addition to this traumatic background, Sally is constantly seeking people, events and experiences to be continually traumatized by. She regularly comes into work declaring that she hates all people. She is moody and toxic. Marianne feels Sally is sucking out every ounce of joy and happiness from the people in the office. Unfortunately, Marianne doesn't feel she has the right to say something to Sally because she believes that this would make her look like a bad person who doesn't care. In reality, Marianne needs to establish a boundary with Sally. Marianne needs to let Sally know that she is sorry for whatever wrongs she has experienced in the past but that Sally needs to leave all of this at home when she leaves for work each morning. Marianne needs to tell Sally that she needs to show up at work in a good mood, even if she has to fake it and to stop terrorizing everyone in the office.

If Marianne established a boundary for all employees that stated that everyone must leave their personal life at home, come to work to do their job, be in a reasonable mood, work well while at work and interact with others in a civilized manner, everyone would benefit. In setting this boundary, this operating instruction, everyone in the office would benefit. As well, this boundary may also prompt Sally to seek whatever help she needs to move forward in a more healthy way. Or, it may prompt Sally to leave her current job in search of an environment that will support her toxic ways.

By Marianne choosing not to have a boundary around this employee's behavior, everyone in the office is suffering. Marianne needs to understand that by doing nothing, everyone is suffering. Marianne wanted to be seen as a nice, caring and understanding person and so she tolerated a less-than-workable working environment. The office was joyless, exhausting and draining. When women struggle to set boundaries or have operating instructions in place, it enables offenders to continue with toxic behavior that makes it difficult for everyone else to cope with. Without firm operating instructions in place, offenders are never required to be accountable for their intrusive behavior.

Operating instructions are not about controlling other people. We are not meant to control others, even young children. People don't like being controlled. The point in having operating instructions is to let people know how to successfully interact with you. They are free to choose to engage with you or not. Even young children choose to engage or not. Unfortunately for young children, their very survival depends on you, so they will do what they can to figure out your operating instructions so that their basic needs will be met. If you are very controlling, as your children get older they will find ways to engage with you less and less.

A handy way to think of a boundary is to think of it as your purse or handbag. As women, we understand that generally everything in my purse is mine and not yours and everything in your purse is yours and not mine. I don't expect to have to carry your purse. You don't expect to have to carry mine. You can't demand that I carry your purse. I can't demand that you carry mine. I don't have the right to rummage through your purse. You don't have the right to rummage through my mine. In fact, I won't tolerate you rummaging around in my purse and you won't tolerate me rummaging around in yours.

As women, we all understand that you might need me to hold your purse for a short period of time and I might need you to hold my purse for a short period of time if either of us has something going on that we can't handle if we are each carrying our own purse. We all understand that for a short period of time we are okay to carry other people's stuff in our purse if we have the space, it isn't too heavy and it doesn't overly burden us. We also understand that we each get to decide what to carry in our purses, how big the purses are and the style and color of the purses. As well, we all understand that I don't get to organize your purse because I think you don't keep it organized enough and you don't get to organize mine. I understand that you don't need me to tell you how to organize your purse, even if it seems to me that your purse isn't being organized properly and I have a great way to keep mine organized. As women, we understand that I don't need your permission or approval and you don't need my permission or approval to change our purses, organize them, keep them messy, dump them out or fumble around in them.

In addition, I'm not offended if you decide to remove something from your purse to lighten your load and you aren't offended if I decide to remove something from my purse to lighten my load. You don't see it as selfish if I remove something from my purse that isn't fitting well in there and I don't see it as selfish if you remove something from your purse that isn't fitting in well.

What if your purse was a symbol for your life and your boundaries? What exactly does your purse contain? It contains everything that is yours. It contains everything you are responsible for. Your purse contains your operating instructions for your interactions with others. These instructions need to be clear. They need to say, "I like it when you do this. I don't like it when you do that. If you do this and it crosses my line, my action will be...."

As I said before, boundaries are multidimensional. They have several components and several layers. Your purse contains your full responsibility for your physical space, including your physical body and your physical environment. No one else can establish boundaries for you in these areas and if they could, you probably wouldn't adhere to them anyway. Or, they may not establish boundaries that keep you safe. It is up to you to keep your physical body free from harm and it is up to you to keep your physical environment healthy and safe.

Your purse contains your full responsibility for your mind and your thought processes. Nobody can make you think a certain way although you can be led to think in a certain way if you aren't aware of your thinking. Your purse contains your full responsibility for all of your emotions, including your happiness. No one else is responsible for any of your emotions. No one is responsible for your happiness or unhappiness. How you feel is up to you. People can't make you feel one way or another. How you choose to respond in any given moment is totally your own responsibility. Have you given this responsibility away to someone, expecting that person to make you feel a different way? Do you believe it is your spouse's responsibility to make you happy? Is it your children's responsibility? This responsibility belongs in your purse, within your boundaries. It is easy to blame others for how we feel but the truth is that how we feel, what we feel and how we respond are entirely under our own control.

Given that you have full control over how you feel, it is a really good thing that this responsibility belongs in your purse and not at the control of someone else. This should give you great comfort. If you don't like what you are feeling or how you are feeling or how you are responding to something, you can change that. If this was under someone else's control, you might be stuck living a miserable life while you wait for that person to change how you feel, what you feel and how you respond. Although it can be quite scary to realize that you have full control over your emotions and responses because you have always expected someone else to be responsible for these, it is quite liberating as well. If you get nothing else out of this book except the understanding that your emotions are your responsibility and they belong in your boundaries that alone will change your life.

Your purse contains your full responsibility for your psychological well-being, which is about bringing congruence to your conscious mind and your subconscious mind and behaving in ways that allow for that. Your purse contains your full responsibility for your psychic well-being. The psychic aspect of you pertains to forces and processes that are beyond your physical and mental awareness and comprehension and have a real influence on your life.

Your purse also contains all of your dreams and desires and your truth. These are your responsibility. These are all part of the spiritual level of boundaries. Our spirit is the life force that animates our physical body. Your dreams and desires and your truth are all part of expressing your soul and why you are here on earth.

Where in your life do you need to let others carry their own purse (life)? Your children, especially your grown-up children? Your co-workers? Your spouse? Your extended family members? School committee members? Where in your life do you need to carry your own purse? Where in your life do you need to stop trying to organize someone else's purse? Who do you need to tell to stop trying to organize your purse? What do you need to take out of your purse to make it easier to live with? What activities do you need to remove from your purse to make your life easier? What are you carrying in your purse that is not yours to carry? What are you carrying in your purse that no longer serves you? Why is it still in your purse? What have you put in your purse temporarily that has become a permanent part of your purse? What do you need to let go of in your purse that is weighing you down? Do you need to be more protective of your purse to ensure that harmful people aren't messing around in it? Do you need to keep certain people out of your purse to keep yourself safe? Do you need to pay attention to what is actually going on in your purse? Do you need to be more responsible for your purse? Are you expecting and demanding everyone else to carry your purse? Is your purse a catch-all for everyone else's junk and garbage? Do you need to be more careful about what junk ends up in your purse? Have you organized your purse lately? Are you happy with your purse? Do you need stronger limits on who gets to be in your purse?

When you understand what boundaries are – internal and external operating instructions for your interactions with yourself and others, your responsibilities, your dreams and desires, and your truth - you realize the question, "Do you have the right to set boundaries?" is ridiculous. Not only do you have the right to set boundaries but it is a requirement for healthy interactions and a healthy, fulfilled life. It is because we generally don't understand what boundaries are that we would even ask that question.

Ultimately, having boundaries allows you to live in the energy of ease even if there is chaos going on around you. You no longer need to jump into the swamp. Why set boundaries? The short answer is to be free; not of your responsibilities and your purse but of all of the people and behaviors that prevent you from feeling joy. Boundaries allow you to be free of the demands of others. Boundaries allow you to be free of the emotional manipulation by others. Boundaries allow you to be free of being taken advantage of. Boundaries allow you to be free of the fear of believing your needs will never be met. Boundaries allow you to be free of intruding in the lives of others. When you set boundaries, you allow yourself to move toward the energy of joy. With joy as the reward, why wouldn't you want to set boundaries?

2

Mother Energy™, Daughter Energy™ and Woman Energy™

Crystal Andrus coined the terms Mother Energy™, Daughter Energy™ and Woman Energy™ to describe the different archetypes that women embody. These archetypes have nothing to do with your age or whether you have children. Regardless of your age, you could be in Daughter Energy because that strategy has served you well throughout your life and it was supported by your family dynamics growing up. Or, you could easily be in Mother Energy even though you don't have any children but you were raised to be in that energy. One of my sisters lives her life in Daughter Energy and she always has. Our parents were quite willing to indulge that behavior and my sister continues to attract people into her life who are active participants in that behavior.

I, on the other hand, was raised to be in Mother Energy. My mom lived her life that way and expected me to do the same. Because I didn't know any better, I became that, and when my mom passed away I just naturally stepped into her shoes and continued on with her unhealthy ways. I had been so well groomed for this energy that it was who I was.

Throughout history, women have essentially had only Mother Energy and Daughter Energy models through which they lived their lives. These archetypes were imposed on women and women were rewarded by society for fulfilling these roles. Only in the last hundred years or so have women been able to embody a new energy. This new energy is the Woman Energy.

Generally speaking, we predominantly live our life in one of the two expected archetypes. We often fluctuate between both sides of this archetype as we interact with different people. As I mentioned earlier, I grew up to be in Mother Energy. I was strongly in Mother Energy - Taken Advantage of for all of my interactions with my mom while she was alive. As well, for 20 years of my life, I was so busy taking care of my mom's needs when she was sick and being taken advantage of by her that I really didn't have time for other people.

After years of dealing with my mom's life-threatening illnesses, I became conditioned to expect a major crisis around the next corner. Because of this, I was pretty much in Mother Energy - Intrusive with most everyone in my life. I didn't have the time or the energy to help people out in a productive manner and I didn't have time to wait for them to ask for help. I got to the point where I would pretty much push someone out of their life when their life wasn't going well. I just pushed people aside, fixed their issue, whether they wanted the help or not, and got back to caring for my mom. I didn't have the time or the energy for someone to have a crisis because I was so busy looking after my mom's needs. I resented it when other people's lives were falling apart. I would ask myself, and sometimes the person whose life was in crisis why they couldn't just hold it all together like I was supposed to do. Dramatic life events can cause us to behave in ways that aren't healthy.

Although we are generally in one of the expected archetypes, unless we are anchored in Woman Energy, we can move in and out of the other energy as we go through the day. For example, you might be predominantly in Mother Energy but a certain relationship or experience pulls you into Daughter Energy each time you interact with that individual or have that experience. On the other hand, you might naturally be in Daughter Energy but a person who is highly demanding might force you to step into Mother Energy for the duration of the interaction. A universal law of physics is that energy is always seeking balance. Unless you are in Woman Energy, different relationships, interactions, environments, expectations and experiences will require you to drop into the other energy in order to keep the energy balanced.

3

What is Mother Energy™?

Women in Mother Energy are the dependable, caring, doing, responsible, protective, rescuing women that we turn to in a crisis. They put everyone's needs before their own and feel selfish if they take time for themselves. They make excuses for the poor behavior of others. Women in Mother Energy feel desperate to be needed. Mother Energy says, "I will take care of you because you can't take care of yourself." A woman in Mother Energy often has no interest in sex because it is just one more thing to take care of and she is tired of taking care of others.

There are two sides to Mother Energy and both of them are unhealthy for you as a woman. The first side is the selfless doer. This energy is Mother Energy - Taken Advantage of. The woman in this energy is always available to take care of everyone's needs. She is dependable, reliable and the one everyone turns to when they need help. Everyone can count on this woman to rescue them and bail them out of their crisis. She prides herself on being the dependable one. She can fix every situation. She is the first person everyone calls when they need something. This makes her feel special.

The problem with this side of Mother Energy is that this woman is an enabler. She enables others to be irresponsible for their own lives. She enables others to never experience the consequences of their actions and choices. They know that she will always take care of whatever goes wrong for them. She will always bail them out of their mess and they never have to learn how to bail themselves out or not get into that position in the first place. With this woman around, people – her spouse, her kids, her friends, her family, her co-workers – never have to do anything for themselves. This woman always wonders why things don't change for those around her and why they don't learn from their mistakes or poor choices. The reality is there is nothing for them to learn because it is only this woman who experiences the pain of other people's mistakes or poor choices. This pain leads to the woman feeling exhausted, numb and resentful.

The woman in this side of Mother Energy wonders why she is always filled with resentment and why she is always exhausted. It has been so long since she identified her own needs let alone met them. This woman is fuming on the inside and can't understand why life is so hard for her when it doesn't seem so hard for other women. She wonders what is wrong with her. She can't seem to say no to people. She likes feeling needed and she doesn't want to offend others by saying no. This woman is often the reason for other people's success but she has no space in her life for her own dreams and in fact, her dreams are long forgotten. This side of Mother Energy is sinister to you because you are being manipulated and taken advantage of by others. Your needs don't matter to you and they certainly don't matter to others.

My mom was 7 years younger than her middle sister and 14 years younger than her oldest sister. My mom was 2 years old when her oldest sister died, leaving just my mom and her middle sister growing up. My grandmother had cancer for most of my mom's life and my grandmother passed away when my mom was only 26 years old. My aunt, my mom's only remaining sibling struggled in school and she dropped out when she was in grade nine. My grandmother was concerned about my aunt's ability to take care of herself and had my mom promise to make sure she was okay after my grandmother passed away. My aunt would be identified today as having a lower IQ but she has always been cunning like a fox and a master manipulator.

When I was 2 years old, my family moved from Montreal to Calgary but my aunt remained in Montreal. Less than two years later, my aunt moved from Montreal and "temporarily" moved in with us. She was supposed to stay with us no longer than 6 months while she found a job and a place of her own. She ended up living with us for 15 years. My aunt was this negative, dark force in the house. She knew she was taking full advantage of her sister and her sister's family and she knew that she had stayed long past her welcome, yet she stayed anyway. My aunt is a Daughter Energy - Entitled woman. She is a demanding, ungrateful, entitled, selfish, self-absorbed, hateful woman who used us, stole from us, robbed my mom of her sanity, caused a lot of conflict in the house and filled the house with a whole lot of hostility.

My mom didn't feel or believe that she had the right to ask my aunt to leave because of the promise she had made to her mother to make sure her sister was taken care of. This promise my mom made to her mother became a noose around my mom's neck that slowly killed her.

My mom had a massive heart attack when I was 19. Mom was 50. Fortunately, she survived this. My mom would have three more heart attacks before she passed away at the age of 71. When my mom was recovering from the first heart attack, my aunt still expected my mom to do for her what she had been doing prior to this illness. My mom would get up early every morning and drive my aunt to the bus so that my aunt could catch it to get to work. In the winter, this meant that my mom would get up, go outside and warm up the car and scrape the windows in preparation for driving my aunt. My aunt never helped with any of this and my mom didn't feel like she could require it of my aunt. After my mom's first heart attack, my aunt still expected my mom to follow their regular routine and scrape the windows even though my mom was unwell and my aunt was perfectly healthy. My aunt never did anything to help out. After all, she was entitled.

Two and a half years after my mom's first heart attack, she finally had the courage to force my aunt to move out. Even then, my mom lied and told my aunt that she needed to find her own place because my parents were moving away from the city. After my aunt moved out, my mom told her that the "job" which required the move had fallen through. My mom needed to say NO to the promise demanded by her mother to take care of her sister. Had my mom said no in the first place, she wouldn't have gone on to have 42 years of complete misery. Don't let this happen to you.

My mom was full of rage. She was being taken advantage of at every turn by her sister and felt there was no way out of this situation. It wasn't like my aunt was mentally handicapped. She was simply a woman who wasn't that book smart and was fully invested in living in Daughter Energy- Entitled. When my mom passed away, I phoned my aunt to let her know that her sister had just died. My aunt's only response was, "Who will take care of me now?" I think my mom ultimately passed away as a way to establish a finite boundary around all of this. My mom is no longer being taken advantage of.

As much as Mother Energy – Taken Advantage of is sinister to you, the other side of Mother Energy is sinister to others. This is Mother Energy - Intrusive. This side of Mother Energy is manipulating and intrusive. A woman in this side of a Mother Energy busies herself in other people's lives and not in her own. When this woman operates from this side of Mother Energy, she is operating on the belief that other people are broken and need to be fixed. Assisting others is always with the energy that they need to do it her way. This woman believes that she knows what is best for everyone around her. She is always surprised that the people around her don't know what is wrong with them. She believes that if they just followed her advice and did things her way, their lives would be so much better. This woman can't understand how people can't see that what they are doing and how they are living is wrong. She can't understand why people don't have the desire to change their lives and she feels that it is her responsibility to fix everyone's "mess".

This side of Mother Energy has the energy of "I can and will make your life so much better and you better appreciate what I am doing for you". This is the "I will fix you" energy. When a woman is in this side of Mother Energy she feels underappreciated and that no one cares about her and what she has so selflessly done for others. A woman in this energy is offended all of the time. She does things that no one asks her to do and she can't understand why no one appreciates her efforts. A woman in this energy uses guilt as an emotional weapon.

The problem with this side of Mother Energy is that people, whether it is your children, your spouse or partner, your co-workers, your friends or your other family members generally don't appreciate being thought of as broken. This does nothing to support their greatness. It is very damaging to those around her, especially to her children when a woman walks around with the attitude of "I have to do it for you because you aren't capable of doing it yourself." Or, "I don't trust you to do it right." Or, "I will have to do it again because you aren't able to do it right the first time so I might as well just do it right the first time." Do you really want the people in your life to believe you feel they are incapable or incompetent and can't do things for themselves? How would you feel if you believed others felt this way about you?

Elizabeth is in her forties. As I was describing Mother Energy and Woman Energy to her, Elizabeth shared a situation about a friend of hers. This woman, Mary, is also in her forties. Mary had a medical issue that wasn't being resolved. Elizabeth was trying to tell Mary what to do and how she should handle the situation. Elizabeth felt exasperated for two reasons. First, Mary wasn't listening to Elizabeth's suggestions or advice and she wasn't doing what Elizabeth was telling her to do. Second, Elizabeth felt exasperated because she was slowly moving into Woman Energy without really knowing it and to use her words, she felt she shouldn't have to parent her forty-something friend. Elizabeth felt Mary should know better and take appropriate action.

I explained to Elizabeth that Mother Energy - Intrusive is all about telling people how to live their lives and that if people just did everything you said, their lives would be so much better. Elizabeth definitely understood this way of being. She said that Mary often complains that every time Elizabeth jumps in to "fix" her, Mary feels belittled and diminished. I said to Elizabeth that that was true. When you jump in to fix someone, that person does indeed feel diminished. This person also feels that the Mother Energy - Intrusive woman sees her or him as broken and incompetent.

Elizabeth was surprised when I told her this. She simply thought Mary was hypersensitive. I said, "No. Mary isn't being hypersensitive. She feels like you see her as broken." This was quite a revelation for Elizabeth. Elizabeth hadn't realized until that moment that when she jumped in to fix the situation or practically demanded that people do things her way for their own good they felt diminished and invalidated. That is exactly what Mother Energy - Intrusive does. It diminishes and invalidates others.

If you feel that setting boundaries is selfish, ask

yourself how is it selfish to step into Woman Energy out of Mother Energy - Intrusive and move away from seeing others as broken? Who is this being selfish to? Yourself? The "broken" person? How can seeing others as broken be unselfish? Moving into Woman Energy and away from Mother Energy - Intrusive is a great gift to you and to others.

I explained to Elizabeth that Mary needed to find her voice and take a stand for herself with her health care providers and find a solution to her health issue. By not jumping in and demanding Mary do everything Elizabeth's way, Mary would be required to find her own way. This would help Mary move into self-sufficiency and true security.

Mother Energy - Intrusive is manipulating and intrusive to others. A woman in this energy never gives the people in her life the space to live their lives. She feels threatened when someone else is successful because this person may no longer have time for her and she will be left out. This is a very controlling energy. Generally women who are in this energy feel that their lives are out of control, so they start to control everyone and everything in their life in order to bring some order back to their life. The reality is, though, that you can't control everything or everyone and people resent you for trying.

If you are in Mother Energy - Intrusive, ask yourself, "Why isn't my life interesting enough to be an active participant in it? Why do I feel I only have value if I am busy in the lives of others and merely an observer in my own life?"

Those who want you to rescue them have no desire to change. They simply want you to bail them out of their current mess and be ready to bail them out of their next mess. Those who truly want to develop mastery, like your children, appreciate your support when it is asked for but really resent you seeing them as broken and in need of fixing.

Both sides of Mother Energy are exhausting, debilitating, draining and joyless. Being in Mother Energy depletes you and takes your attention and intention away from you moving your life forward. Mother Energy is very heavy, dense energy. Women in this energy often end up wearing this density on their bodies in the form of extra weight.

Note: Crystal Andrus coined the term Mother Energy™. The additional descriptions of Mother Energy - Taken Advantage of and Mother Energy – Intrusive are my terms and are not affiliated with Andrus's work.

4

What is Daughter Energy™?

Daughter Energy is all about you. Whereas Mother Energy is all about others, either being taken advantage of by others or fixing others, Daughter Energy is "What's in it for me? What can you do for me?" Women in Daughter Energy feel desperate to have their needs met. Daughter Energy says, "You need to take care of me because I can't do it for myself."

It is not as though women in Daughter Energy are unsuccessful. Many are successful. It is just that they expect people to carry their purse – do projects for them at work, be responsible for their happiness, etc. Women in this energy have a singular focus of getting others to be responsible for them and to take care of them. Every relationship they enter is viewed with this singular focus: will you be responsible for me and take care of me and to what extent?

Just as there are two sides to Mother Energy, there are two sides to Daughter Energy. The first side is the manipulating side. This energy is Daughter Energy - Entitled. This woman is self-absorbed, irresponsible, selfish and manipulative. This is the high maintenance woman who expects everyone to be at her beck and call to make her life easier. She is always having a crisis, which she expects and demands that someone else fix. She acts helpless and needy. She thinks she is entitled. She is often "daddy's little girl" even as a grown woman and "the princess". She uses her moods as a weapon against others. She often has tantrums and lashes out at people. She never takes responsibility for her emotions or her outbursts because everything that happens is someone else's fault in the first place. She constantly wonders how everyone can be so thoughtless. Encounters and interactions with these women can be very painful.

A woman in Daughter Energy - Entitled is too consumed with her own needs to pay attention to what is going on around her. She never helps out when someone else is going through a crisis and she doesn't care how her behavior impacts others. After all, people are in her life simply to make sure her needs are met.

A woman in this energy is never happy when someone else has success. This woman resents others being successful because it takes the spotlight off of her. She is resentful when someone else's life is going well. A woman in this energy will often shut you out of her life for a period of time. This side of Daughter Energy is abusive towards others.

Joy was about to have a baby. Joy's parents, Celia and Van, lived 300 km away and would be retiring in a few months. Celia and Van wished to be closer to their daughter and new grandbaby. They decided that they would move to where Joy lives. Joy was delighted with this decision and started looking for a home for her parents to purchase in her city. Joy found a wonderful condo for her parents in a 55+ community. This would have allowed Celia and Van to be close to Joy and her family as well as having a community of people who were at the same stage of life. Joy placed an offer on the condo, which was accepted.

Everything went along nicely until Joy's sister, Ellie, who lives with her husband and son on the other side of the world, heard about the place that her parents were buying. The condominium association rules stated that because the building was for people who were 55 years and older, no one under that age could live there but they could stay for a brief period of time.

Ellie, in full-on Daughter Energy - Entitled energy, asked her mother, Celia, where she, her husband and her son would stay if they ever moved back to their home country and needed to move in with Celia and Van until they got their own place. If Celia and Van bought this condo, then Ellie and her family wouldn't be able to live there *if* they ever moved back to their home country. Ellie also asked Celia where her 8 year-old son would stay, if in 10 years from now, he decided he wanted to attend university in Celia's city.

Celia became worried that she would be denying her daughter and her family a place to live if they ever moved back to their home country. Because of this worry, Celia and Van decided to back out of buying this condo. This required Joy to seek legal services to get out of the purchase agreement. Joy had to spend more time searching for a suitable home for her parents that could accommodate her sister and family should they ever decide to move across the world.

This is a very good example of the manipulative Daughter Energy - Entitled behavior and the

"What's in it for me?" and "If I'm not happy I will make sure everyone adjusts to make me happy." mindset. Everything needs to work for Ellie or other people need to make changes to their plans to suit her. It didn't matter to Ellie that the likelihood of her being required to live at her parents' place was very remote. In Ellie's mind, her parents' new living arrangement didn't work for her so her parents needed to make the change necessary so that it would work for her.

Normally Celia operated in Daughter Energy – Entitled and expected everyone to take care of her and make her life easier. However, with Ellie so strongly in Daughter Energy – Entitled this required Celia to be in Mother Energy – Taken Advantage of with Ellie. Celia was afraid of being shut out of her daughter's life, as women in Daughter Energy - Entitled often do to people they want to manipulate. Celia was afraid of being rejected by Ellie. This fear was sufficient to cause Celia to change her plans.

As mentioned above, Celia was generally in Daughter Energy - Entitled and she exhibited this with her daughter, Joy, who was in Mother Energy – Taken Advantage of. Not once did Celia and Van come to Joy's city to look for homes for her and Van. Celia left all of the house hunting to Joy to take care of. This was manipulative on the part of Celia and Van. They expected Joy to put in the time and energy to find a house that Celia and Van would like. If you are buying something as significant as a house, shouldn't you be the one who is searching for it to determine if it meets your needs? Celia and Van needed to take responsibility for this and not place this responsibility with Joy. If Joy ultimately bought a house that didn't meet the needs of her parents, she would always be blamed for the inadequacies of the purchase.

As well, if Celia and Van were truly serious about moving to Joy's city, they would put in the energy and effort required to make this so. Celia and Van were in their sixties. They were healthy, vibrant and mobile. They should have been doing the house hunting as part of their preparations for their major life change. If they weren't serious about the decision to move to Joy's city, they needed to own that and stop leading Joy on.

Some women in Daughter Energy- Entitled are very devious. They seem like they are doting mothers all the while other people are always looking after their children. They seem like they are interested daughters-in-law and actively engaged with their in-laws because this interaction is enjoyable all the while they are only interested in what their in-laws can do for them, financially, with child care or with whatever resources they have to their avail – free vacations, vacation homes, expensive gifts and the like.

These women are very polished and very practiced at coming off as women in Woman Energy. We look at them and marvel at how calm they are and how they seem to have everything together all the while they spend as little time with their children as possible. They seem like women we want to become. If we go below the surface, though, we would find a joyless woman who is bored with her life, tired of her tedious in-laws, and wants to escape to a place where her demanding, selfish ways could simply be on display. If this woman was truly in Woman Energy, she would radiate joy and magnetism. We would want to be with her more because it feels good to be around her.

This woman knows how to craftily take full advantage of the Mother Energy - Intrusive woman who craves to be needed by her adult children. This woman knows how to do that without seeming to be doing that. She gives this Mother Energy - Intrusive woman the attention that she craves and allows her to do all kinds of things for her – take the grandkids for the weekend, take her shopping, buy her expensive gifts and clothes, pay for vacations with her and her family so the Mother Energy - Intrusive woman can spend time with her grown sons. This woman seems to be a gracious host and yet when you leave the event that she was hosting, you feel like you had an interaction with a porcupine. The encounter was prickly; all the while, the Daughter Energy - Entitled woman smiled and calmly interacted with you.

This woman is shallow and plastic meaning that she will become whatever personality her husband or partner or important people in her life require her to be. She offers no opinions on anything and she simply echoes what the important people in her life espouse. Very little is authentic about this woman.

It is fascinating to watch this woman ply her craft. Watching her from afar is like watching a spider spin a web. She mesmerizes her "prey" with her calm demeanor and skillful manipulation and then she spins her web around the prey, making it very difficult for the prey to escape because its need to be needed is fulfilled by this skillful spider. If you are this woman, ask yourself, "What part of me is authentic?" Just my inner pain? My need to be taken care of?

While Daughter Energy - Entitled is abusive toward others, the other side of Daughter Energy is abusive toward the self. This is Daughter Energy - Self-Abusive. A woman in this energy is terrified that her needs will never be met. She compares herself to other women and feels less attractive or less successful or less worthy or all of these. This woman is prone to self-abuse through various ways including eating disorders, excessive shyness or by being excessively sexual. She believes that no one will or can love her. She is full of fear.

If she is in an intimate relationship, she starts to freak out if the sex wanes because this is the only way she believes she can keep her partner interested in her. She believes that in order for her partner to be interested in her she needs to have sex all the time. She has no idea how to have her needs met in a healthy way so she uses sex as a way to make this happen. If there is no sex, the relationship is over. Sex is the only way women in this side of Daughter Energy feel valuable in a romantic relationship. No sex = no value. No value = no longer taken care of.

Women in this energy often have many intimate relationships, always looking for a partner who will take care of them. Women in Daughter Energy - Self-Abusive are afraid to live on their own. Some of these women even moved in with their boyfriends when they were still in high school. Because of this fear, they often put up with all kinds of abuse from their partner.

Melissa was 14 when she first started having sex. She had very little self-esteem and was looking for validation from teenage boys. Melissa dropped out of high school in grade 11 and moved in with her first boyfriend when she was 17. She felt helpless and needy. Melissa married this man when she was 19. Her husband was physically, emotionally, mentally and psychologically abusive to Melissa. Melissa left the relationship a couple of times only to go back to her husband each time. She finally managed to leave her husband and make a new life for herself.

Melissa moved to a new city and married a new man. This relationship lasted for five years and was the start of a pattern for Melissa. Being needy and demanding comes with a price. Melissa's husband found this behavior to be exhausting, he walked out on her and requested a divorce.

Melissa met and moved in with a new man. This man turned out to have Bipolar Disorder and had violent mood swings. Unfortunately for Melissa, she got pregnant. She was now needy, demanding and responsible for a child. She and this man parted ways.

Melissa was always having a crisis from which her mom always bailed her out. Melissa had no desire to become self-sufficient or secure and it wasn't being demanded of by her mom. Melissa's mom was heavily invested in her own Mother Energy – Intrusive energy which allowed Melissa to remain in her Daughter Energy – Self-Abusive energy.

Melissa simply expects others, especially men, to take care of her. She is in her fifties now and has been married five times. Melissa has no viable plan for retirement. She is living with a man who is retired and living on a pension. Should Melissa still be with this man when he dies, she will be left with nothing as everything this man has will be left to his adult children. Melissa will end up on the streets.

Note: Crystal Andrus coined the term Daughter Energy™. The additional descriptions of Daughter Energy - Entitled and Daughter Energy – Self-Abusive are my terms and are not affiliated with Andrus's work.

5

What is Woman Energy™?

What exactly is Woman Energy? The archetypes of Mother Energy and Daughter Energy identify women who feel powerless and are constantly afraid that their needs will never be met. A woman in Woman Energy is none of these. She is centered, strong and empowered. She feels powerful inside. This isn't a "power over you" energy but a "powerful within" energy. She knows what her needs and desires are and she is capable of meeting her needs and pursuing her desires. This isn't a selfish energy, but a self-full energy. A woman in Woman Energy is present in her own life and she is fully engaged in it. Women in both Mother Energy and Daughter Energy are not present or engaged in their own lives.

Mother Energy - Intrusive and Daughter Energy - Entitled are both selfish energies. Mother Energy - Taken Advantage of and Daughter Energy - Self-Abusive allow others to be selfish. Woman Energy is neither selfish nor does it allow others to be selfish. A woman in Woman Energy collaborates with others and does so with ease. She embodies the energy of joy, allowing, receiving and intuition. She feels safe in the world. This woman is authentic and magnetic to be around.

Mother Energy is a "giving to prove" energy. A woman in this energy is always giving in order to prove she is worthy and valuable of someone else's time, energy, attention, recognition, approval, friendship or whatever else this woman is seeking. Daughter Energy is a "taking" energy. A woman in this energy takes whatever is being demanded or offered – time, energy, attention, money - and she takes all of it. Unlike the giving to prove energy of Mother Energy and the taking energy of Daughter Energy, Woman Energy is "gifting and receiving" energy. A woman in Woman Energy realizes that she has nothing to prove and she isn't interested in fulfilling someone else's requirement that she prove herself. Instead of giving to prove, she gifts everything. A woman in Woman Energy gifts her time, energy, attention, focus, talents and abilities.

Giving is the opposite side of the same coin as taking, and it has an unpleasant feel to it. When you give something, there is an implied taking – someone is taking from you. As well, there is an attachment energy to giving. You never fully release what is being given, so there is always an expectation of getting in return. Gifting, on the other hand, is free of attachment. When you gift something, you release it and it is free to be received or not. There is no expectation of getting when you gift. A woman in Woman Energy understands that gifting is an expression of freedom and contribution. She knows that she has talents and abilities that benefit her and others and she shares these in ways that move her closer to fulfilling her desires. A woman in Woman Energy understands that having dreams and desires is an important part of the human experience and that pursuing these dreams and desires makes her a valuable example for other women to follow.

Women in both Mother Energy and Daughter Energy are victims. They are victims of their circumstances. They are victims of the demands of others and being shut out of other people's lives. There is no power in being a victim. Women in Woman Energy don't see themselves as victims. They see themselves as powerful, influential, purposeful and self-directed.

Women in both Mother Energy and Daughter Energy live in the energy of fear. They fear saying no. They fear letting people down. They fear being shut out of people's lives. They fear not being needed. They fear not being able to do things for themselves. They fear not being loved. They fear not having their own needs met. There is a very damaging physiological effect of constantly living in fear. When you feel fear, your flight or fight response is activated. This means that cortisol, the "stress" hormone, and adrenaline, the "let's get going" hormone, are released in the body when the brain registers a threat of some kind. The body is designed to release these hormones when we face something scary or dangerous and these hormones are designed to get us quickly away from danger.

There is no difference in your body between physical danger such as when you are about to be hit by a car and mental, emotional or psychological danger. All of these experiences trigger the release of cortisol and adrenaline. The problem, however, is that unlike a physical danger, which has a starting point and an end point in terms of being in danger; mental, emotional, and psychological experiences generally have a starting point but no end point. They continue to be felt in the body as though they are still happening, long after the initial event. This means that cortisol and adrenaline are constantly being released in your body.

Although adrenaline, or epinephrine as it is medically referred to, is life saving in situations that require it, any amount of it in a woman's body in non-crisis time is very harmful. As women, we thrive with oxytocin flowing through our bodies. This leads to a "tend and befriend" state and allows us, as women, to feel safe, connected and trusting. The tend and befriend state does not mean tending and befriendding others. It refers to tending to yourself and befriending yourself so that you are in an optimal state of well-being.

A woman in Woman Energy is in an oxytocin state. She is calm and centered and her physiology supports this. A woman in Woman Energy lives in the energy of ease. Ease is a vibration that is above the density of drama. Ease does not mean easy. Easy is an expectation. Expectations lead to disappointment. Ease, on the other hand, is an overarching energy that allows you to stay out of struggle. There will always be challenges – whether it is the challenge of learning something new, or the challenge of interacting with difficult people or the daily challenge of traffic – but when you are in the energy of ease these challenges don't take you down. You meet each challenge with a greater calmness and with a knowing that this will be accomplished without lots of drama or struggle. Even tasks that initially feel overwhelming or even dreary will be accomplished in a calm, steady manner. Women in Woman Energy live in the energy of ease and set the intention daily to be in this vibration and to be in the space of ease with every activity they begin. Women in Woman Energy bring this ease, this lightness, this calmness to everything they do.

Woman Energy is expansive energy. Every experience helps a woman in Woman Energy feel more expanded. Every experience helps her grow and become more joyful and more open to opportunities. It is a self-full energy. When a woman is in Woman Energy life feels hopeful and optimistic.

Mother Energy and Daughter Energy are constrictive energies. Whether you are doing too much for others, taking over the lives of others, demanding others take care of you, or are harming yourself in some way, you are being constrictive. Your life is smaller because of this and you feel suffocated by this. You have no joy in your life and your life feels overwhelming and hopeless.

A woman in Woman Energy is in an optimal balance of her feminine and masculine energies. People throw these words around like they truly understand the meaning of them but they often can't properly explain them. Energetically speaking, feminine energy is the flow. Masculine energy provides the structure. Think of feminine energy as the river and masculine energy as the riverbanks. We are made up of both these energies and they need to be in balance in order for us to be healthy and vibrant. We need strong riverbanks to give structure to our flow and give our flow direction. As well, we need strong flow in order to move our lives forward. Regarding boundaries, think of boundaries as the structure that allows your flow to be directed in ways that support your highest version of yourself.

Some women have way too much masculine energy in their bodies. These tend to be women in Mother Energy. Women who have too much masculine energy generally achieve what they want to achieve through force. They push and push and push until they achieve the desired results. For women, force is exhausting and depleting. Physiologically speaking, women do not thrive in the energy of force. This is an adrenaline state that leaves women feeling depleted, bitchy, defeated and exhausted.

Some women tend to have way too much feminine energy in their bodies. These tend to be women in Daughter Energy. Women with too much feminine energy generally achieve what they desire through starting this and jumping over there to start that and then stopping and starting and stopping. They require the structure provided or imposed by their circumstances or by others. This structure is often resented and resisted. All of this effort and resistance leaves women exhausted and depleted. This, too, is an adrenaline state which, as mentioned above, leaves women feeling depleted, bitchy, defeated and exhausted.

A woman in Woman Energy has sufficient structure for her energy to flow optimally and she has sufficient flow for her life to move forward well. For the first time in history, women are being called to step into Woman Energy to become the joyful, confident and strong individuals that we are.

6

Mother Energy™, Daughter Energy™, Woman Energy™ and Boundaries

What do Mother Energy, Daughter Energy and Woman Energy have to do with setting boundaries? Earlier I talked about how boundaries can be thought of as your purse. Since we, as women, identify strongly with a purse, I will use this term throughout this section. When it comes to your husband, your son, a male friend or male colleague, think of it as their gym bag instead of a purse. With regards to carrying one's purse, the first side of Mother Energy, Mother Energy - Taken Advantage of, says, "I will carry your purse because I don't have the right to say no to your expectation of this." The other side of Mother Energy, Mother Energy – Intrusive, says, "I will carry your purse because I don't think that you can do that for yourself."

The first side of Daughter Energy, Daughter Energy - Entitled, says, "I expect you to carry my purse because I am entitled to this and I am too lazy or disinterested or important to carry my own purse." The other side of Daughter Energy, Daughter Energy - Self-Abusive, says, "You have to carry my purse because I am so fractured that I can't carry it myself."

Woman Energy says, "I will carry my purse. You will carry your own age-appropriate purse. I will help you, if I have the resources available - time, energy, money, attention units, etc. - if you are experiencing a burden or crisis, and if doing so fills me up because I am able to gift my time, energy, attention, money or other resources. I don't do this out of obligation or out of resentment."

Why does this matter? If you think about boundaries and setting boundaries from this perspective, you will have a framework that gives you a very clear way to decide whose purse you are carrying and why. When you are in Woman Energy and you are carrying your own purse and allowing and expecting everyone else to carry their own age-appropriate purse, you are in a very "powerful within" mindset. This mindset is the mindset of true security.

True security exists
when all needs can be met by the self.
– *Sanaya Roman*

When you stand within this circle, you can evaluate every request, behavior, interaction, relationship or experience to see where that would put you with regards to your circle. Will this request, behavior, interaction, relationship or experience require you to carry someone else's purse? Will it require or demand someone else to carry your purse? Are you assisting someone or are you carrying them or taking over their life? Will it pull you outside of Woman Energy and back into Mother Energy or

Daughter Energy? The point of establishing boundaries is to stand in Woman Energy at all times. Woman Energy becomes the Master Boundary. It is an energetic circle that you stand in and it centers you. It contains everything you are responsible for including your physical requirements, your feelings, your likes and dislikes, your desires and dreams, and your truth. You feel secure because you know that you can fully meet your own needs.

This doesn't mean, however, that you have to do everything by yourself. It means that you understand that you are responsible for yourself. You are responsible to ask for assistance. You don't expect people to read your mind and "just know" that you need support. It means that you say no when it doesn't serve you to say yes. It also means that you reach outside of yourself and say yes when you would normally say no.

When you are in this circle, you understand that in order for others to respect you, you have to respect yourself first. When you are in this circle, you understand that it is necessary for you to live your life in a way that pleases you, instead of living a life that pleases others and tramples you in the process. It also means that others get to live a life that pleases them without you demanding something from them or without you guilting them into something. It means that you value yourself enough to develop trust in yourself and to develop mastery. It means that you take care of for yourself what you would normally expect others to take care of for you. When you are in this energy, this essence, this circle, you understand that standing in your truth gives others permission to stand in their truth. When you are in this energy, you know that there is no guilt because you are standing in the essence of who you naturally are – self-sufficient, powerful within and truly secure.

None of this means you don't care about anyone but yourself. It simply means that you see yourself as secure. It means that you see others as competent and capable of self-sufficiency. It means that you respect your time, your energy, your resources and your dreams. It means that from the day your children are born, you see them becoming self-sufficient and having the ultimate security – being able to meet their own needs. It means that you have the power within to protect your time, your energy, your resources, your truth and your dreams. You are not counting on or demanding that someone else do this for you. As well, you are not taking over someone else's life to do it for her or him.

Being in Woman Energy means that you do not allow yourself to be taken for granted or taken advantage of. You do not allow yourself to intrude into other people's lives. You are a full participant in your own life. You do not fling your emotions all over the place. You do not expect others to be responsible for your feelings, especially for your happiness. You understand that you are responsible for that. You are not self-abusive. You believe you are a woman of value and worth.

As you feel centered in Woman Energy and feel the peace of that centeredness and the ease of this, you will come to understand that this circle, this essence, this energy is the Master Boundary. Everything within it is yours. Everything outside of it is not yours.

It is important to note that I am not saying that as a mother in Woman Energy you don't take care of your kids, especially if your kids are young. What I am saying is that you need to raise your children from the Woman Energy perspective. You want to raise your children with the intention of them becoming self-sufficient adults who can take care of their own needs and have true security. You want to raise your children so that they are encouraged to carry their own purses. You want to encourage them to find solutions to their problems. You don't expect them to carry your purse. You allow them to have friends and you are their parent who provides the limits and allows them to set their own boundaries that are respected. You allow your children to try and fail and try again. You don't jump in to do everything for them before they do things for themselves. You encourage mastery. You give them choices so they feel the effects of good choices and good outcomes and bad choices and bad outcomes. You allow them to develop trust in themselves. You have expectations of them carrying their own, age-appropriate purses.

You don't make them responsible for your happiness. You don't tell them that you used to have dreams but now they take up so much of your time that you have long forgotten your dreams. You pursue your dreams and your desires to show your children that it is important and necessary to live a fulfilled life. In Woman Energy you raise your children always with the intention of them becoming self-sufficient and always with the understanding that true security for them comes from being able to meet their own needs when they are adults.

Even with young children, you are not responsible for their feelings, their desires or their dreams. As a woman in Woman Energy, you are responsible for providing love and the resources necessary to ensure your children are in a safe physical environment and that you are meeting their basic physical needs. As well, you are providing an environment that supports their mental, emotional, psychological, psychic and spiritual needs *and* you constantly and persistently have the intention of your children growing into self-sufficient adults who have dreams and desires that they need to pursue.

Woman Energy encapsulates all of the aspects of boundaries. It holds the physical, mental, emotional, psychological, psychic and spiritual spaces and contains all of your responsibilities. With Woman Energy as the Master Boundary, joy is not only possible but it is a given. Being in joy is truly your soul's reason for you being in human form.

SECTION TWO

Boundaries and Living Life on Your Terms

7

Is Guilt Necessary?

Guilt seems to be an epidemic these days, especially for women. It seems like we are supposed to feel guilty for just about everything. Even worse, we feel we are supposed to feel guilty if we feel that we aren't feeling guilty enough.

The general definition of guilt is that it is an emotional flag letting us know when we have done something wrong so that we can change our behavior and either make amends for our wrongful behavior or learn from it and not do it again. Based on this definition then, guilt is an emotion that is based on the past. It seems that as a society, we weren't satisfied with guilt being an emotion that speaks to the past. We somehow decided that we need to use guilt as an emotion that we also fling into the future. Now we are supposed to feel guilty for things we haven't even done yet. It is as though we need to punish ourselves today for what we haven't even done yet. Yikes!

There are two kinds of guilt. The first is called "appropriate guilt". This guilt serves as a moral and behavioral compass, ensuring that we make amends for what we did wrong and learn what not to do in the future. This type of guilt is useful, hence the term "appropriate". The second type of guilt is "inappropriate or unhealthy guilt". This is the guilt we feel when we believe other people feel we should be doing things differently. It is called "inappropriate guilt" because what we are doing isn't something that requires the emotion of guilt. It is this type of guilt that we fling into the future. We get into the headspace of thinking, "Oh my goodness, if I do this (whatever it is), *she* (your mother, your friend, the committee member, your co-worker) or *he* (your husband, your father, your manager, the preacher) will think I am a bad person for doing it or for doing it this way." This type of guilt creates all kinds of crazy for you. More importantly, this type of guilt is a really big distraction that keeps you from doing what your heart and your soul are longing for you to do. We fear losing approval or attention or acceptance or whatever else by doing the activity.

With guilt, you walk around wondering, "What will the world think of me in the future if I do something my way or do something in a bigger, bolder way or if I become more or if I say no to a socially expected and accepted behavior or way of being?" Guilt also says, "You shouldn't want more for your life than your parents experienced. You are greedy if you desire more." You walk around with the sense that you won't be okay being more than you are right now. You also start thinking, "Do I have the right to do this in this way?"

Guilt is like a "should". You should do this. You should do that. Who says? How does it feel to should all over yourself? It kind of feels like crap. You can't live a fulfilled life if you are crapping all over yourself. The real problem with guilt is that women use it as a way to hide out from living a fulfilling life and we use it on others to prevent them from living a fulfilling life. Because guilt is concerned with the beliefs of others, we get a lot of buy-in from others that taking this action or that action is wrong and therefore we shouldn't be doing it. Guilt is a contractive energy that gives us permission to remain stuck and unhappy. A lot of women are quite content to remain stuck and unhappy and therefore guilt suits them quite well.

Guilt is a choice in the sense that you can choose to stay in the emotion of guilt or you can choose to move out of it and possibly remain out if it. You won't change this simply by choosing not to feel guilt. Instead, you have to change your programming around this. Some guilt is conditioned into us. A lot of us grew up in households where guilt was used as an emotional weapon to keep us in line, especially by women in Mother Energy – Intrusive energy. For most of us, guilt is an automatic response that we drop into because we are expected to feel this way and because it is a part of our subconscious programming.

Depending on the subconscious programming and what trapped emotions women have, some women can't choose to move out of guilt. The programming and trapped emotions keep them stuck here. What they can choose, however, is to want to change this stuckness. By releasing their trapped emotions and changing the guilt programming in their subconscious minds, they are able to then make the choice to move out of guilt. Choosing to step out of guilt is an operating instruction for *you* and it is something you require to have a boundary around. Guilt is a lower vibrating emotion that keeps you from being the greatest version of yourself. Moving out of this emotion is a powerful way to move your life forward.

The first step in choosing to move out of guilt is awareness. If you aren't aware of your guilt patterns, you won't be able to change them. Awareness precedes action and awareness precedes a shift. Are you aware that you are feeling the emotion of guilt? Is this a go-to emotion for you when you start to think about good things happening in your life or how you would do things differently? Are you aware of whether you want to remain in guilt or if you are ready to move out of guilt? Be okay with where you are at. If you are feeling guilt and you want to remain in that emotion, own it.

Don't resist what you are feeling. Simply allow yourself to feel what you are feeling. Know that you have the right to feel whatever you are feeling and that you can stay in whatever emotion you are feeling for as long as you like.

Next, ask yourself why you are feeling guilt. Is this an automatic response for you? I have heard Dr. Christiane Northrup, a leading expert on women's health, say on many occasions that if your mother isn't happy, she will make sure you remain at that same vibration along with her. Is guilt the emotion that keeps you at your mother's level of happiness? Is it the socially expected reaction and you are simply feeling this way to fit in with society's expectations? Are you a bad person if you don't feel guilt in this situation? Is it bringing your attention to a subconscious program that needs to be released? Is it giving you permission to hide out and not step forward into whatever you desire to step into? You will gain some incredible insights into this emotion when you go through this step.

Now, ask yourself how you would like to respond in the future in this type of situation. Is there an emotion you can feel that isn't so contractive? Is it safe to feel this new emotion? What else is coming up for you here? This awareness will help you move beyond the guilt that you are feeling.

Guilt is an approval-based emotion. Because of this, you will need to change the subconscious programming and trapped emotions you have around needing approval. Subconscious programming is very powerful. If your programming says that you don't have the right to want more, become more, receive more, you will feel guilty for desiring those things. Your programming will make it virtually impossible for you to let go of the guilt because you are supposed to want to remain where you are at and you are supposed to feel guilt about this.

We toss the term "subconscious mind" around a lot these days without really understanding what it is. The subconscious mind is a part of the mind that acts like a tape recorder. It records everything that has happened to you. It is a stimulus-response system. It is responsible for 90 to 95 percent of your reactions and behavior.

For the first seven years of your life, your mind operated in a hypnotic, daydream state. This means that everything was taken in and recorded. So, all of your parents' beliefs about what should and shouldn't happen, their views of the world and their understanding of how things should work, look and feel were all recorded in your subconscious mind and this became your subconscious programming.

The job of the subconscious mind is to keep you safe. It takes every experience you have and evaluates it against what you have programmed into it. If this new experience or interpretation of the experience differs from what you already have programmed in your subconscious, it will get rejected. So, if your understanding of the world, which is really your parents' understanding of the world, which is really their parents understanding of the world, etc., is that you are supposed to feel guilt because you want to live your life differently, then you will feel guilt. Thinking your way to a different reaction won't change this. Releasing your subconscious programming with releasing processes will change this. If you want to have different reactions and different emotions, you have to have different programming.

A woman in Woman Energy understands the importance of reprogramming her subconscious mind so that it supports the emotions she chooses to feel so that she can get out of and stay out of guilt. She also understands that there is no space in her life for guilt. She understands that since she has nothing to prove, she doesn't require the approval of others. A woman in Woman Energy understands that she has the right to live her life on her terms.

8

What Does Stress Have to Do With Boundaries?

If you believe setting boundaries is selfish and that infusing things, people, activities and experiences into your day that please you is selfish, think about this: A 2009 study by Lilianne R. Mujica-Parodi, Ph.D., associate professor of Biomedical Engineering at the State University of New York, Stony Brook, found that when you smell alarm pheromones (the chemicals produced by sweat in someone who has just gone through a stressful situation) in someone else, this can subconsciously trigger the fear center of your own brain even when you aren't going through that stressful situation. According to Mujica-Parodi, alarm pheromones make you more aware of potential threats. It is as if you are in a constant state of high alert, even though it isn't even your stressful situation. This constant state of high alert is a hallmark of clinical anxiety.

As you already know, chronic stress is bad for your health. It puts you at risk of high blood pressure, heart disease and even death. However, picking up on someone else's stress may be significantly more harmful. When someone is upset, their brain reacts at first and then gradually stops responding.

When you react to someone else's stress, you don't become accustomed to the pheromones and your brain doesn't return to the unstressed starting point. The study determined that chronic vicarious anxiety could have a greater effect on you than direct stress. In addition to this, researchers are discovering that children begin to catch another's stress at a very early age. Researchers have come to understand that the more stressed a mom is, the more stressed her baby is.

So, it seems that remaining stressed is the selfish behavior that causes second-hand stress to those you love. If you set boundaries so that you are less stressed, everyone around you will benefit.

Also, if you continue to keep people in your life who choose to live chronically stressed, know that this stress is contagious and is harming you. You have the right to choose for yourself to limit exposure to this person. This isn't a selfish act. It is a self-full act that benefits you and those around you. As you move away from that person, you will be able to start releasing some of the harmful stress that this person was causing you to experience. Your health will improve as will the health of those with whom you spend time.

If this person had a contagious disease, you wouldn't feel selfish staying away from him or her. You would think that it was a smart choice to avoid contact with him or her until he or she was better. The same is true with stress. This stressful person is contagious and you need to make the healthy choice to stay away from him or her as much as you can to avoid picking up the stress. Make this choice for yourself and for your family. If you are that stressful person that others need to avoid, it is time to make different choices for yourself. Setting boundaries that will ultimately lessen your stress will benefit you and everyone around you.

It isn't selfish to give yourself space from the demanding drama queen at work. Regardless of whether this person is your friend, co-worker or manager, spending more time with this person than is essential is harming you. If you are this demanding, drama-filled person, stop being that way. Your stress is making other people sick.

As you move away from these drama-filled people, explain to them, if you wish, why you are doing so. This explanation might help these drama people see the need to change their behavior. If you don't feel comfortable explaining this to them, know that you don't owe anyone an explanation for your boundaries. You have the right to protect yourself in whatever way is necessary.

What do you do if this demanding drama queen or king is your mom or dad, your sister or brother, your adult daughter or son, or your aunt or uncle? Limit your exposure. This might sound harsh and perhaps impossible. After all, this person is your mother or father or sister or brother or adult daughter or son or aunt or uncle. It would hurt them if you put limits on the time you spent with them. Right? What about the hurt she or he is causing you? You have the right to not be in an environment that puts you at risk.

The problem with stress is that people wear it as a badge of honor these days. It seems that everyone "competes" for the title of "most stressed". And, because so much of who we are is tied into how hard we work, it is very difficult to reduce stress. What most people hear when someone tells them that they are too stressed is that they aren't handling things well. The usual response to this is "I'll show you," and the person then takes on more to show that they can handle things.

What a strange world we live in when we believe that being more stressed than someone else is righteous. Think about that for a minute. How does this even make any sense?

In order to reduce stress long term you have to know how you feel and what you believe about stress. If stress is your friend, you are not about to let it go easily. If you have had enough of being stressed, you will let it go more easily. You will establish the boundaries necessary to reduce your stress. A woman in Woman Energy understands that stress is harming her and her family and she willingly establishes the boundaries she requires to significantly reduce her stress levels. In doing so, she is honoring herself.

9

How Does Pleasure Fit With Boundaries?

I recently watched an interview with Dr. Sara Gottfried, author of *The Hormone Cure*, and Dr. Christiane Northrup. In 1994, Dr. Northrup wrote the
groundbreaking book, *Women's Bodies, Women's
Wisdom*. In it she showed that women's most com-
mon physical issues are rooted in what we think, feel
and believe and in the choices we have made. She
also showed that we can have health by listening to
our bodies.

In the interview, Dr. Gottfried asked Dr. Northrup what the number one thing was a woman could
do to balance her hormones. Dr. Northrup's answer
was simple – increase pleasure in your life. When
women hear this, they automatically think it means
sexual pleasure. That can be part of it, especially if
you find sex pleasurable. If you are having sex
purely because your partner expects it, then this
isn't pleasure and if you expect to have sex because
that is how you demonstrate your value, then that
isn't pleasure either.

Pleasure is defined as the state of feeling of being
pleased. It is also enjoyment or satisfaction derived
from what is to one's liking, gratification or delight.
Synonyms, or other words that similarly describe
pleasure, include happiness, enjoyment, delight and

joy. Enjoyment is defined as a quiet sense of well-being. Delight is defined as a high degree of pleasure, usually leading to an active expression of it. Joy is a feeling of delight so deep and lasting that one radiates happiness and expresses it spontaneously. Wow! How can any of these states be seen as selfish? How much better would your life be if you filled each day with activities, interactions and experiences that please you?

We can experience pleasure in many ways. Steeping your favorite tea in your favorite mug can bring pleasure into the moment. Savoring some chocolate can bring pleasure into your day. Just don't inhale back a chocolate bar mindlessly. You will have finished it without allowing it to increase your pleasure.

I live in Canada. As I write this book, there is a commercial on TV that was created by the dairy producers of Canada to promote the consumption of cheese. The creators of this commercial understand this pleasure principle and the commercial is all about making your day and your life better by enjoying something you really like. The voiceover says that we should measure our servings of well-being and grams of enjoyment and have a recommended daily dose of pleasure. The voice goes on to say that pleasure is not a luxury and that it should be prescribed and is the one thing we can use more of. Clearly, someone behind this commercial understands that your day and your life are better when they are filled with what pleases you.

Alicia is beginning to understand this concept. She is a classic example of a Mother Energy woman. She flips between both sides of this energy and she will be in Mother Energy - Taken Advantage of when she is interacting with her husband and friends and in Mother Energy – Intrusive when she is dealing with her grown children. Alicia never expressed her needs or desires. She always put everyone ahead of herself, including the wants and needs of her husband. Alicia had done this for so long that she didn't feel she had the right to express her desires.

Alicia's doctor suggested that she drink a glass of red wine each night, which he felt would give Alicia a certain health benefit. Alicia's husband bought expensive wine and loved to lavish guests with a fine bottle whenever he and Alicia entertained. Alicia felt that since her husband loved to share his expensive wine with guests, he would have no problem with her having a glass of this wine each night. Alicia's husband thought differently. He had cheap wine available for Alicia. Alicia, who has been married for a long time, was deeply hurt by this selfish display by her husband. The good thing for Alicia was that she was moving out of Mother Energy and into Woman Energy as this wine experience was going on and she understood the concept of doing things that pleased her. Alicia identified her desire for a nice glass of fine wine and she went out and bought her own wine and kept it for herself to enjoy.

Alicia could have remained hurt and angry in Mother Energy and allowed herself to believe that she didn't deserve to have fine wine. Instead, Alicia chose to take care of her own needs and desires and infuse pleasure into her day by buying and drinking wine that pleased her.

This story demonstrates two really important concepts. First, Alicia took a stand for herself and declared that she was worth having something she enjoyed. She valued herself enough to spend money on fine wine and not settle for a cheap bottle. Second, in doing this, Alicia allowed herself to infuse something that pleased her into her daily routine.

Think about the things you enjoy and how they increase your feelings of pleasure. It could be spending a few minutes outside in the sunshine. Or, perhaps you delight in reading and you haven't picked up a book (or downloaded one) in a long time. How would it feel to read a few pages today? Maybe taking the time to paint your toenails brings you pleasure or it would please you to go for a pedicure and have someone else paint your nails. Would having fresh flowers on your desk at work add to your level of pleasure? Perhaps you would enjoy fresh flowers on your kitchen table or on your bathroom counter. If so, buy some for yourself. If you believe that fresh flowers should only come from your spouse, you are going to spend a lot of time waiting for someone else to enhance your pleasure.

When you operate from Daughter Energy and you expect everyone to take care of you and your responsibilities, and to carry your purse, you can't infuse pleasure into your day because you are always expecting others to do this for you. This leads to terrible disappointments. For starters, the people you demand this from may not have any desire to indulge this. If they are willing to indulge this, they may have absolutely no idea what pleasures you expect. They may have no idea what pleases you because you have no idea what pleases you. You have to know what pleases you first and you need to be the one who infuses these pleasures into your day and your life.

Would it increase your sense of pleasure if your kids made their beds or if your spouse or partner did the dishes after supper or if you stopped bailing your grown children out of their situations? Having boundaries such as requiring your kids to make their beds, wipe the toothpaste out of the sink, come to dinner when called and whatever additional activities are required are simple acts that may bring great pleasure into your day. How can these boundaries be selfish?

As you increase the amount of pleasure in your day and your hormones start to become more balanced, your mood will improve. As your mood improves, everyone around you will be positively impacted. How is this selfish?

As a society, we have bought into the notion of "no pain, no gain". This is actually a harmful belief, especially for women. This mindset says that to move forward, it must hurt first. Feel into this for a minute. Does this way of thinking even inspire you to take action? It doesn't inspire me to take action. I don't want to experience hurt before something good comes my way.

The truth is that we can only build up our capacity for pleasure. This builds up a reservoir of energy we can use in times of difficulty. We cannot, nor should we want to, build up our capacity for pain. If you increase your capacity for experiencing pleasure, you will be able to cope more easily when something painful happens and you will be able to recover faster when the painful experience is over. If your life is devoid of pleasure, you don't have much energy available to deal with life's valleys.

Do at least one thing every day that pleases you. Keep adding to this so that you get to a point where your day is filled with pleasure. The delight of this will help you feel lifted up. Build up a reservoir of pleasure and delight. This will keep you centered when life knocks you off balance.

If we think about boundaries as carrying our own purses, how does the concept of pleasure fit in? There is pleasure in carrying your own purse. There is pleasure in not getting stuck carrying someone else's purse. There is pleasure in saying, "This activity pleases me and when you do that, it displeases me." There is pleasure in being fully responsible for yourself. There is pleasure in expecting and requiring everyone to have age-appropriate responsibility for themselves.

A woman in Woman Energy understands the principle of pleasure and infuses pleasure into her daily life. Pleasure is a part of her way of being.

10

Is it Selfish to Say NO?

If living your life in a way that pleases you balances your hormones and balanced hormones increase your health and well being, how can this be selfish? How is it selfish to be responsible for your own emotions? How is it selfish to be responsible for your own dreams? What a strange world we live in if we believe that walking around filled with resentment and bitterness isn't selfish but being lit up living a life that pleases us and feeling fulfilled is selfish.

The problem isn't that it is selfish to have boundaries. The problem is that if we do have boundaries, we can't blame others if our life isn't working well and we can't blame others if we have no idea what our desires are.

What we are really saying when we ask if setting boundaries is selfish is that we are afraid of becoming the manipulating woman in Daughter Energy - Entitled. Whether we are predominantly in Mother Energy or Daughter Energy, we have all encountered the woman who puts herself above all others without any regard for how her actions, words or behaviors make others feel. This woman is in a selfish, constrictive, "what's in it for me" energy. Interactions with her suck the life out of you.

Compare this to the woman in Woman Energy who is infusing her day with actions, words, behaveiors and things that please her. When we encounter a woman who infuses her day with pleasure, we want to become more of that. This is an expansive, light-hearted energy that radiates out and that others feel pleasure in being around. You can't be this woman if your day and life are filled with people, activities, and requests that drain you, suck all of your energy away and leave you feeling depleted.

Is it okay to say no because the request you just received would take time, energy and focus away from something that pleases you? Is the world made better when you say yes to a request that makes you highly resentful and therefore causes everyone around you to become irritable because they are feeding off your resentment energy?

What if you receive a big request or expectation like caring for your parent (or a sibling, relative, friend, or committee member) as she/he recovers from an illness? Will you be providing this care from a place of pleasure or from a place of resentment? It is possible that providing this care, even though it would drain you entirely of your own emotional, mental, physical and psychological energy, would be deeply pleasing to you. It is also possible that providing this care would make you incredibly resentful and hostile. If you can say yes to this care because it pleases you, then everyone benefits. If you say yes to this care because you don't want to appear selfish but in doing so makes you incredibly hostile, then no one benefits. Your energy will be drained out of you and not easily replenished because you will be filled with resentment. The person you are caring for will always feel this resentment. This isn't the kind of energy that will assist the person in getting well. People who are going through major life challenges need people who can and will lift them up, not drag them down. If you said yes in this situation, everyone loses.

Amy should have said no but instead she said yes. Amy's mother, Judy, was 70 years old and owned a retail store. The store was quite successful and Judy loved owning it and running it. She ran the store by herself with the assistance of employees, none of whom were family members. Unfortunately, Judy suffered a massive stroke. Not only was Judy no longer able to run her store, she was also no longer able to live on her own and take care of herself.

Instead of allowing arrangements to be made for assisted living, Judy decided that she would rotate through her three daughters' homes and have them provide the care she required. Judy would spend a week at the first daughter's home, a few weeks at the second daughter's home, and whatever amount of time she could be tolerated at the third daughter's home. This, in itself, was an overwhelming situation for Amy. Amy knew that every few weeks her mother would be dropped off at her house so that Amy could provide care for her. Who wants to be the one to say no to one's mom?

To add to this, Amy was now required to run Judy's store. As much as Judy loved her business, Amy had equal contempt for being required to run the store. Amy had absolutely no interest in the store. She was filled with resentment and hostility toward her mom. This resentment and hostility began to fill every part of Amy's life. Her personal life was turned upside down with her mother's rotating living arrangements. Her work life was turned upside down by the expectation of running her mom's store. All of this negative, depleting energy was draining Amy and draining the store. The store went from being a profitable business to bankrupt in a couple of years.

Amy thought she was doing the right thing by saying yes to her mom and no to herself. Ultimately, Judy would have been better served if proper living arrangements had been made for her right after her stroke. Judy required a level of care that her daughters couldn't properly provide and ultimately didn't want to provide. If Amy had sought a buyer for Judy's store right after Judy's stroke, when the store had vitality and profitability, Judy would have netted a financial gain instead of a disastrous financial loss. Everyone involved in this situation thought that saying no to Judy was selfish when in fact saying no would have been the best course of action.

Instead of feeling like she had the right to say no and establish some boundaries with her mom, Amy reluctantly said yes to what turned out to be a monumental disaster. She felt like a failure for not keeping Judy's store running profitably. Her marriage was now struggling because Amy was so consumed with her mother's needs. Amy had little time for her own family and she was so filled with resentment and hostility that her home had become filled with that energy. This was taking its toll on Amy, her husband and their children. Saying yes in this case was self-destructive for Amy and everyone lost out with this decision.

When a situation like Amy's occurs, lots of people will tell you that you should take care of the person in question and that doing so is such a great thing. The people who say these things are never the people who actually provide the care. They have no intention of ever stepping up to provide this care. They have too many "important" things to do in their own life. They have no idea how demanding and draining this care is and they don't know how much of your life you will miss out on by providing this care. Don't listen to these people. Know that you have the right and the permission to say no to this request or expectation. Also know, to your core, that you are not a bad person for doing so.

If you do say yes, know that you don't have to do all of the work yourself. You can and should ask for support from others. Asking is critical, though. People aren't mind readers. Generally speaking, a lot of people want to step up and support you through a crisis or demanding experience, but they simply have no idea what you require. Asking for support and assistance is not a sign of weakness. It is truly a sign of strength and an acknowledgement that you want to honor yourself during this trying time.

Life is a team sport. We all need the support and assistance of others to be our greatest selves. Even highly successful solo athletes don't do it alone. They make it to the top because they have teams of people who contribute to them to make it all happen.

A woman in Woman Energy doesn't expect to do it all by herself. A woman in this energy understands that asking for support and assistance is not an act of weakness but an act of self-care and of self-honoring. She also understands that she can receive support without feeling obligated to give in return. As I mentioned earlier in this book, a woman in Woman Energy gifts her time, energy and resources which frees her from the attachment of whether something is received. It also frees her from the expectation of someone taking from her or from her having to give in return. A woman in this energy isn't a taker. She isn't taking from someone and she isn't expecting people to carry her so when she needs support and assistance, she is free to receive this and gifts support freely. Because she carries her own purse, a woman in Woman Energy doesn't take advantage of people. However, she has their backs in a way that doesn't leave her depleted. Assisting others in a time of need doesn't mean you take on their purse. It simply means that you lighten their purse.

If you are one of the women who never steps up in a time of crisis, it is time to do so. Anne was 21 when her fiancé, Anthony, was in a serious motor vehicle accident. Anne was at work when it happened and Anthony's mother phoned Anne at work to let her know. She left work right away to go to Anthony. Anne was at the hospital for two hours before Anthony's parents showed up. Anthony had smashed both of his knees into the dashboard during the accident and had surgery on them a few hours after Anne arrived. Anne left to go home and waited for the call that Anthony's surgery was finished. Anthony was operated on into the night and was in recovery early in the morning. Anne went back to the hospital to find out how everything went and how Anthony was doing. Anthony's father was there, but there was no sign of his mother. This would be a recurring pattern during Anthony's month-long hospital stay. Days would go by without Anthony's mother going to the hospital to visit him. Anne went every morning before work and every evening after work.

Anthony lived at home with his parents at the time. When he got home from the hospital, he required several weeks of bed rest as well as doctor appointments and extensive physiotherapy. His parents didn't take him to one appointment. They expected Anne to drive over to their house, pick him up, lift him into the car (he had two full leg casts on), take him to his appointments, bring him back home, get him up the stairs and back into the house. This went on for weeks. Anthony's parents even went away on weekends and expected Anne to stay over to take care of him while they were away. According to Anthony's mother, "It was all just too much to cope with." If you haven't figured it out yet, Anthony's mother is a classic Daughter Energy – Entitled woman who is selfish, asks what's in it for her and expects everyone else to do the hard work.

Anne was drowning in exhaustion. This type of care is depleting, exhausting and overwhelming. Anne was afraid that if she didn't provide the care to Anthony then he wouldn't be cared for. She didn't know at the age of 21 that if she said no to this, it would require others to have to say yes.

If Anne hadn't provided all of the care to Anthony, someone in his house would have had to. If Anthony's father had been required to figure out how to do this, he would have required Anthony's mother to step up or they would have hired out this care. Either way, Anthony would have received the care he needed and Anne wouldn't have had to do it all on her own.

Your children require you to step up, whether it is for everyday parenting if your children are not adults or for a major crisis regardless of their ages. The people close to you require you to step up as well. It is time to do so. You don't get to be the selfish princess with no backbone and no sense of commitment to others. As a parent, you made this commitment to step up the moment you decided to become a parent. Beyond your children, you make this commitment every time you establish a close relationship with someone.

What I don't think women in Daughter Energy understand is that by not stepping up, they are risking the entire relationship they have and will have with their children or other important people in their life. Part of being successful in a relationship is the knowing by both parties that the other person has your back in the time of need. When you don't step up, you erode this trust. Once trust is lost, it takes a monumental effort to rebuild it. Many people won't give you the opportunity to even try.

Anthony has a very cursory relationship with his mother. She eroded all of his trust in her. Anthony interacts with his mother only when he is socially required to do so. He will speak with his mother when she calls but almost never calls her. Anthony was deeply wounded by his mother's selfish behavior in his time of need and he has little regard for her. Anne has no relationship with Anthony's mom. Anne has no respect for her and she has no interest in being manipulated by her. Anthony's mother lost out

on the opportunity to build a special relationship
with Anthony and with Anne.

11

Mother Energy™, Daughter Energy™ and Your Health

There is a really good reason to move out of either Mother Energy or Daughter Energy and into Woman Energy. Being in either Mother Energy or Daughter Energy can contribute to health issues. Everything is energy and everything has a vibration and everything has a resonance. Every organ in your body has a healthy vibration. Anything that goes on in your body that has a lower vibration can cause the vibrations of your organs, and everything else in your body for that matter, to decrease. Lower vibrations in your body lead to dis-ease and potentially to disease. Your thoughts are energy. Your emotions are energy. Lower vibrating thoughts and emotions cause your body to be unhappy.

Louise L. Hay wrote a groundbreaking self-healing book in 1984 that identified the underlying mental and emotional causes of physical issues. Her book, *Heal Your Body*, identified patterns of thinking, feeling and behaving that lead to dis-ease in the body, which if not released lead to disease in the body. For example, if you walk around in Mother Energy refusing to nourish yourself physically, mentally, emotionally, psychologically and spiritually;

put everyone else first; over-mother; overprotect and are overbearing; you are setting yourself up for breast problems including cysts, lumps and soreness. Or, if you go around acting and reacting like a little kid full of Daughter Energy you could end up suffering from kidney problems. The entire book is a listing of physical ailments and the underlying mental, emotional or psychological issues.

I have listed some of the physical issues here along with the corresponding mental, emotional and psychological patterns so that you can get a sense of what I am talking about. According to Hay:

Ankle Issues: Inflexibility and guilt. Ankles represent the ability to receive pleasure.

Arthritic Fingers: A desire to punish. Blame. Feeling victimized.

Cellulite: Stored anger and self punishment.

Heart Attack: Feeling alone and scared. "I'm not good enough. I don't do enough. I'll never make it." Squeezing all of the joy out of the heart in favor of money or position, etc. Lack of joy. Belief in stress and strain.

Hip Problems: Fear of going forward in major decisions. Nothing to move forward to.

Knee Problems: Stubborn ego and pride. Inability to bend. Fear. Inflexibility. Won't give in.

Menopause Problems: Fear of no longer being wanted. Fear of aging. Self-rejection. Not feeling good enough.

Osteoporosis: Feeling there is no support left in life.

Karol K. Truman wrote *Feelings Buried Alive Never Die*. The premise of the book is that unresolved feelings can create havoc both in your emotional well-being and in your health. In the back of her book, she has a list of physical issues and the underlying thoughts and beliefs that brought these issues forward. I have included some of them here. According to Truman one or more of the underlying thoughts or beliefs contribute to the physical issue.

Anxiety: Feels unable to "call the shots" in life. Feels boxed in. Feels helpless to affect a change.

Arthritic Hands: Rigid, perfectionist or controlling personality. Severe self-criticism and criticism of others. Inflexible, feelings repressed and mirrored in the hands.

Back Problems: Feeling no support. Can't cope with emotional difficulties. Feeling burdened emotionally. Feelings of frustration. Wanting someone to "get off my back".

Back – upper
Withholding love from others. Feeling agitated or anxious.

Back – middle
Feeling guilty. Lacking self-support. Lacking in self-confidence.

Back – lower
Feeling unsupported financially. Experiencing fear where money is concerned. Wanting to back out of something. In a relationship that hurts. Running away from a situation.

General Aches: The feeling of being all alone. Feeling that nobody loves me. Aching to be held and loved. Feelings of sadness.

Hardening of the Arteries: Fears being disappointed. Hard hearted. Being dictatorial. Feeling obstructed or delayed in life. Unresolved feelings obscuring the flow of life. Perfectionism.

High Blood Pressure: Feels a strong need to be in control of everything. Allowing situations or people to bother you. Letting your emotions and reactions bother you. Not minding your own business or interfering with others.

Shoulder Issues: Bearing burdens that don't belong to you. Life is too great a burden to bear. Carrying stressful responsibilities. Lacking courage.

(Interesting note – if your purse (either or both your physical purse or/and your metaphorical purse) is too heavy you will experience shoulder issues as well.)

Sinus Trouble: Trying to call the shots in someone

else's life. Dominating possessive. Being irritated by someone close to you.

Stomach Problems: Our sense of security feels threatened. Fear of new ideas. Lack of affection. Condemning the success of others. Unhappy feelings.

Swollen Ankles: Feeling overworked but can't quit. Feels there is no relief from pressures in life.

Ulcers: Worrying over details. Conflict as to capability. Frustration at not having things go the way you want. Pressures too much to bear. Feelings of anxiety, fear or tension. Seeking revenge. Feelings of conflict or helplessness or powerless.

Urinary Infections: Putting blame on others for your problems. Allowing another to irritate you.

Yeast Infections: Deep and unresolved resentments. Lack of self-love. Inability to claim one's own power. Unable to love and support the self. Unable to accept the self. Not recognizing your own needs.

Dr. Alex Loyd, N.D., Ph.D. created a healing system called *The Healing Codes™*. This process heals the underlying beliefs that cause physical conditions. Dr. Loyd identified that specific negative emotions, negative beliefs and harmful actions lead to certain physical conditions and diseases.

If your pattern is Mother Energy - Taken Advantage of and you have the negative emotions of rejection, hurt and fear; the unhealthy beliefs of "People will take advantage of me. People are too sensitive;" and you engage in the harmful actions of doing things to gain the approval of yourself and others; then according to Dr. Loyd, your Central Nervous System would be negatively impacted. This means that you could experience headaches, numbness, viral infections, loss of sensation in one or more of the five senses, loss of brain function, or loss of spinal cord function. The negative emotions, unhealthy beliefs and harmful actions listed above lead to conditions such as Attention Deficit Disorder, Alzheimer's disease, brain fog, dementia, glaucoma, hand tremors, Lou Gehrig's Disease (ALS), meningitis, Multiple Sclerosis, Parkinson's Disease, stuttering, tinnitus, and vertigo.

If your pattern is Mother Energy - Intrusive and you have the negative emotions of guilt, shame, wrongful pride and envy; the unhealthy belief of "People must think well of me in order for me to be okay"; and engage in the harmful action of manipulation, then according to Dr. Loyd, your circulatory system will be negatively impacted. This means that you could experience irregular heartbeat, blood clots, lymph congestion and tissue swelling. The negative emotions, unhealthy belief and harmful action listed above lead to such conditions as aneurysm, atherosclerosis, congestive heart failure, hypertension, general swelling and varicose veins.

If you are a woman operating from the pattern of Daughter Energy - Entitled and you have the negative emotions of laziness, entitlement, and helplessness; the unhealthy beliefs of "I can't do it. I'm not capable. Others should do it for me. It's not fair."; and engage in harmful actions including manipulation, deceit and giving up; then according to Dr

Loyd, your muscular/skeletal system will be negatively impacted. This means that you could experience fractures, bone demineralization, cartilage wear and tear, aching joints, or arthritis. According to Dr. Loyd, the negative emotions, the unhealthy beliefs and the harmful actions listed above lead to conditions such as bunions, bursitis, Carpal Tunnel Syndrome, cataracts, fibromyalgia, hernia, osteoporosis, plantar fasciitis, repetitive strain injury, sciatica and tendonitis.

If your pattern is Daughter Energy - Self-Abusive and you have the negative emotions of unforgiveness, insignificance, resentment and jealousy; the unhealthy beliefs of "I am unlovable. I am insignificant. I am flawed."; and engage in the harmful action of self-protection, then according to Dr Loyd, your endocrine system will be negatively affected. This means that you could experience changes in your thyroid function, hormonal problems, low sex drive, increased inflammation, decreased ovulation and changes to your insulin levels. The negative emotions, unhealthy beliefs and harmful action listed above lead to conditions such as amenorrhea, anorexia, bulimia, Chronic Fatigue Syndrome, diabetes, endometriosis, hypertension, obesity, PMS, sugar cravings, and weight issues.

Important note: Dr. Loyd and *The Healing Codes*™ are not connected with the concepts of Mother Energy, Daughter Energy or Woman Energy. I am simply showing the connection between these archetypes, the underlying beliefs and emotions of these archetypes and the physical conditions that result from these beliefs and emotions as outlined by Dr. Loyd.

From these different healing concepts created by different individuals, it is clear that having thoughts of being overburdened or unlovable or feeling incapable, overly critical, over-mothering, powerless or being filled with resentment, anger and hostility are detrimental to your health and well-being. Reading this section alone should instill in you the understanding that it is important to move into Woman Energy and that carrying your own purse, requiring others to carry their own age-appropriate purses, having the sense of true security of being able to take care of your own needs and allowing and requiring others to do the same is necessary for your own well-being.

SECTION THREE

Key Areas of Your Life That Require Boundaries

12

Should You Set Boundaries With Your Children?

Is it selfish to set boundaries with your children? A lot of women believe that it is. I was watching Joel Osteen on TV one day recently. Joel is a non-denominational pastor with a weekly television show. His broadcast is simply of his weekly message. This particular show was titled "Healthy Families." He made an interesting comment about boundaries to all of the parents listening. He said that when children have boundaries set for them and parents set limits on their children's behaviors, then children understand that they are loved. Osteen went on to say that when you, as a parent, set limits on your children's behaviors, but not, however, on their dreams, you are letting your children know that you care enough to do that and that they matter enough for you to care.

The opposite of this is true as well. If you don't set limits on your children's behaviors and don't have expectations for them, children interpret this to mean that you don't care enough to do that and they don't matter enough for you to do so. Think about that the next time you think setting boundaries is selfish. Boundaries tell your children that you care about yourself and you care enough about them and that they matter enough to you for you to establish limits. Do you love your children? Do you want them to feel loved? Do you want them to feel like they matter and that you care? Do you want your children to thrive? If so, set boundaries for them.

A woman in Woman Energy understands that not only does setting boundaries with her children, young or grown-up, help them feel loved and valued, it is also a way for her children to balance their masculine and feminine energies. As I mentioned in the chapter on Woman Energy, masculine energy is the structure and feminine energy is the flow. Boundaries provide the structure and direction for your children's energy to flow optimally.

Do you allow your children to have their feet up on the kitchen table? Seems like a strange question, doesn't it, because who would allow this? Well, as I was writing this chapter, I was eating lunch on a patio and a woman in her early twenties a table over from me had her bare feet up on the table and it wasn't because she needed to use them to eat with. She simply felt entitled to do this and had no notion that this was gross and completely inappropriate. I hope you are teaching your children to keep their feet off the table. This is a great boundary and limit that everyone benefits from but clearly a boundary that wasn't insisted upon by this woman's parents.

Your lack of boundaries for your children has an impact on others, not just you. This young woman was clearly in Daughter Energy - Entitled and she simply believed that she could behave any way she chose. If your daughters are in Daughter Energy, stop indulging this. You are not helping them become successful adults. They will always expect that they can do whatever they please and they will always expect other people to do things for them that they need to know how to do and take care of for themselves. Don't raise your daughters to be princesses. They become someone else's burden later on.

It is also important to mention that you don't want to raise your sons to be princes. I haven't mentioned anything in this book to this point about the males in your life. However, just as females can be in Mother Energy, Daughter Energy or Woman Energy, males can be in Father Energy™, Son Energy™ or Man Energy™. You want to raise your sons to be in Man Energy. You don't want to raise your sons to be in Son Energy.

Raising your sons to be in Son Energy, by doing everything for them and treating them like the sun rises and sets on them results in grown-up boys. These aren't the kind of men who have dreams and a vision for their lives. Men in Son Energy are entitled, lazy, and always expect someone to take care of them. This does not make them responsible family men or major contributors to society. Raising your sons to be in Son Energy does not give them true security.

No matter the age of your or children you always need to have the intention of these people growing into self-sufficient adults, even if they are adults already. It is never too late to have this intention. As well, it is never too late to establish boundaries with your children. Even if you didn't have boundaries with your children when they were young, you can establish them now with your grown-up children. Expect and require them to take care of their own needs. Expect and require them to bail themselves out of their "mess". Seeing your children become truly secure because they can take care of their own needs is the greatest gift you can give them.

Having no expectations of your children is significantly more damaging to them than having big expectations for them. When you have no expectations for your children, their subconscious mind interprets that to mean that you don't think they are capable of doing something and you definitely don't believe they can do something magnificent.

I was watching a show one time called something like "Bubble Wrap Kids". This particular episode featured a family of five – mom, dad, and three kids. The oldest child was around 11 years old. The mother was cutting the meat for the three children because she thought it was safest that way and she was afraid her children would get hurt if they each had a knife. When the host of the show asked the oldest child how he felt, he said, "My parents think I am stupid and not capable of doing anything for myself." Wow! Is that what you want your children believing about themselves as they grow up? How does that give them true security – the knowing that they can take care of their own needs as an adult? What are you preventing your child from doing? Growing up? Failing? Experiencing consequences?

I had a conversation with a man named Fred. Fred is a medical professional and has two children. His oldest is a 5 year-old boy. I asked Fred what his expectations were for his son in terms of schooling and his future. Fred's response shocked me. Fred said that he didn't really have any expectations for his son to pursue education beyond high school and that if his son didn't finish high school he would force him to move out and get a job. Here is this man with a medical education who is making a very good living for himself and his family and he couldn't imagine more for his son than to finish high school, maybe. Fred's son hadn't even started school yet, so Fred had absolutely no idea what kind of student his son was going to be but Fred couldn't imagine something bigger for his son than finishing high school, maybe. Imagine how Fred's son feels inside knowing that his dad doesn't believe that he will even finish high school. Why would Fred's son even care to try?

I was totally shocked by Fred's comments. I said to Fred that is was really important for parents to have expectations for their children to do great things. I shared with him this story.

For whatever reason, Joan's parents had absolutely no expectations of Joan, their eldest daughter, to do or become anything. She dropped out of high school in grade 10 and floated around for a few years before she got a full-time, minimum wage job. She has worked at a minimum wage job ever since. Just so I am clear here, I am not saying that there is anything wrong with minimum wage jobs. All work is important and all jobs matter. What I am saying here is that Joan has access to few opportunities and that earning minimum wage gives her very little money to live an expanded life. Joan is now in her fifties. Her life is hard and full of struggle. On the other hand, Joan's parents had very explicit expectations for their second and youngest daughters. They were told from a very young age that they must go to university and complete a degree. Both daughters have completed Master degrees and both have access to opportunities that their oldest sister doesn't. Joan is smart, highly capable and tenacious. Her life would have been a lot different had her parents had expectations for her.

Imagine how your children feel believing you believe they aren't capable of doing anything, whether it is cutting their own food or finishing school. It is incredibly demoralizing to believe that your parents don't think you are capable of much.

It is really important that you have expectations of and for your children and to have boundaries for them. Expect and require them to keep their rooms clean, be respectful of others, look at you in the eyes when you are speaking, wipe the toothpaste out of the sink, help prepare meals, learn to do laundry, do their homework, come to the dinner table with their electronic devices turned off, pay attention at school and achieve their best at whatever other activities will help them become fully functioning adults.

Expectations are critical for children. You don't want to have expectations that are so high that your children will never be able to meet them. However, when you have no expectations of and for your children and you do everything for them, subconsciously they understand this to mean that you don't believe they can do anything. This is emotionally, mentally and psychologically damaging and demoralizing for them.

One of my sisters was an elementary school teacher for over 16 years. We were talking about this topic one day and what she said surprised me. She said that when everything is done for children and they aren't allowed to try things for themselves, they start to believe that everything needs to be absolutely perfect the first time they do try something because you have instilled in them that failure is not an option. This puts enormous pressure on your children.

You can see that happening to children. They are so afraid to fail because they have never been allowed to try and fail and try again that they believe that everything they do has to be done perfectly the first time. This is setting them up for extreme anxiety and overwhelm. Imagine believing that everything you do you have to do perfectly the very first time. How would this make you feel?

Do you expect your children to reach their full potential? Do you expect that your children have no potential? Do you expect that having expectations for your children to reach their full potential will somehow cripple them? This seems to be a real problem these days. A lack of expectations for children is crippling them now. Thank goodness parents don't prevent their children from learning how to walk. Children have an innate desire to walk and will keep trying until their muscles have it all figured out. Can you imagine what your children's lives would be like if you carried them everywhere because you have no expectations of them walking and you simply took over that task? Your children would be devastated.

If you don't have any boundaries or limits at home for your children, how do you expect them to interact properly in a classroom full of children? If you don't provide limits and boundaries on your children's behaviors at home, your child's teacher has to be even stricter at school to compensate. This makes your child's teacher "the bad guy".

The real issue here is that children are constantly seeking boundaries and limits on their behavior. You are not harming them if you have boundaries and limits on their behavior. Limits and boundaries make them feel safe, loved and cared for. That is true for everyone, regardless of their age. We all feel more at ease when we know what the boundaries are for all of the different experiences and interactions we have.

If you are in Mother Energy - Intrusive, don't pretend you are volunteering at your child's school because you feel it will benefit your child. Own the fact that you think you can teach better than your child's teacher. In reality, if that were true, you would be leading the classroom and not the teacher. This is very intrusive behavior. No one is interfering with your work at your workplace. Don't do that to your child's teacher. You have no idea how hard her or his job is. Have you ever gotten 30 or more children to follow instructions at the same time? I doubt it. Let your child learn without your intrusion. If you feel your child requires more instruction, provide it at home.

If you are in Daughter Energy - Entitled, don't expect your child's teacher to be responsible for your child's learning. This is your child's job and yours to ensure that it happens. The teacher provides the environment in which to learn and the information required by your child, but it is up to your child to actually do the learning and it is up to you to make sure your child is learning what needs to be learned.

As important as it is to have expressed boundaries and limits for your children's behavior, it is equally important to have boundaries around your behavior and expectations with your children. These need to be part of your operating instructions for yourself. Do not expect your children to parent you. That isn't their job, nor is it their responsibility. It is your job as their parent to parent them, not the other way around. As well, do not expect your children to be responsible for your emotions, especially for your happiness. This is your responsibility and only you can make you happy. Do not live your life through your children. You are required, as a healthy, vibrant adult to have and pursue your own dreams and desires and you need to expect and give space to your children to have and pursue their own dreams and desires. Your children need you to encourage them to pursue their own dreams and desires, but it is crippling for them to have to pursue something that fulfills your dreams and desires.

Do not make your children feel they aren't smart enough to figure things out on their own. They need your guidance and direction and, equally important, they need the space to work things out on their own. This is how we develop a sense of mastery. We figure things out and we get good at doing that. Mastery is very fulfilling to one's soul. It is essential for living a fulfilled life. You want your children to grow up to have mastery and fulfilled lives, don't you?

As well, do not burden your children with all of your problems. They don't have the psychological development to understand them and sharing all of your problems with them makes their world feel very unsafe. Your problems are yours to solve. They aren't your children's to solve.

What kind of children are you raising? Are you raising children? Or, are you raising adults? I hope you are raising adults. Raising adults means that you always have the intention in everything you do that your children grow up with a true sense of security, knowing that they can take care of their own needs. A woman in Woman Energy establishes boundaries for her children, whether young or grown-up, because she knows that this is in the best interest of her children and in the best interest of herself.

13

Do You Have the Right to Set Boundaries With Your Husband?

Having boundaries with your husband is really critical if you want to live a joyful life together. We, as women, really struggle in this area of our lives. Most of us believe that we aren't entitled to have boundaries with our husbands and most of us have been raised that way. As well, there is an underlying current in society that says that we don't have the right to set boundaries with our husbands.

Julie is in her late fifties. She has been married for over 33 years. She works two jobs. Her full-time job has differing shifts. She is required to work the 6:00 am to 2:00 pm shift a few days a week as well as the 3:00 pm to 11:00 pm shift the remaining days. Sometimes it works out that Julie works until 11:00 pm one night and starts at 6:00 am the next day. This means that Julie gets to bed at 12:30 am or later and gets up four hours later to get ready to go back to work. Julie had a day like that recently. After getting to bed at 12:30 am, Julie got up at 4:30 am to get ready for work, went to work for 6:00 am and worked until 2:00 pm. This was a day that she also worked at her other job. On Julie's way home from her first job, her husband called to ask if she would make lasagna for him for supper. Julie wasn't even going to be home for supper because she would be working at her second job by this point. Julie really didn't want to make this dinner for her husband because she wanted the 1.5 hours she would have at home to simply rest. If you have made lasagna, you know that it takes over an hour to make. Julie never said no to her husband, regardless of the request, because she didn't believe she had the right to. Julie agreed to make the lasagna and leave it for her husband to enjoy.

Julie got home, made the lasagna, cleaned up the kitchen, cleaned herself up and headed out to her second job. By the time Julie got home that night, she had been on the go for over 18 hours with four hours of sleep prior to that. She was resentful of her husband's request for dinner. She felt it would have been much easier for her, and not a hardship for her husband, had she required her husband to pick up something to eat on his way home from work.

I believe we continue to receive opportunities to create boundaries for ourselves until we establish them. As I mentioned at the beginning of this story, Julie is in her late fifties and has always behaved this way. She has been given plenty of similar opportunities to say no and require her husband to fend for himself for a night. It is never too late to establish boundaries and to say no to a request and establish better operating instructions with your husband. It is never too late to teach your husband how to treat you.

A woman in Woman Energy requires her husband to be in Man Energy because all energy seeks balance. If a woman is centered, balanced and powerful within, as is a woman in Woman Energy this requires her husband to be in Man Energy to create the energetic balance.

The other side of this coin is true as well. A man in Man Energy requires, energetically speaking, his wife to be in Woman Energy in order for his energy to be in balance. This is an important point. If you desire your man to be in Man Energy you must be in Woman Energy. If you aren't in Woman Energy, your husband won't be in Man Energy.

As I mentioned in the previous chapter, just as women can be in Mother Energy or Daughter Energy or Woman Energy, men can be in Father Energy™ or Son Energy™ or Man Energy™. As with the terms for women, Crystal Andrus coined these terms for men.

Just as there are two sides to Mother Energy, so are there two sides to Father Energy. The first side of Father Energy is Father Energy - Father Knows Best. Everything has to be done his way because he is the only one who knows how to do things properly. He believes he is more important than you are and he has very little interest in what you have to say and doesn't believe that anything you say has value. His know-it-all attitude is exhausting and invalidating. He is not interested in whatever is upsetting to you because it really doesn't matter. A man in Father Energy - Father Knows Best energy doesn't care that you have dreams and desires and he often thinks your dreams and desires are stupid. He wouldn't desire these, therefore why should you? He expects to be treated like a king. He is demanding, selfish and narcissistic.

The other side of Father Energy is Father Energy - Taken Advantage of. This man feels it is his responsibility to make everyone happy – his wife, his kids, especially his daughters, his manager at work, etc. He over-commits and he can't say no. He is exhausted and depleted and feels he has let everyone down.

Just as there are two sides to Daughter Energy, there are also two sides to Son Energy. The first side of Son Energy is Son Energy - The Son. This grown man is still desperately seeking the approval of his mother and father. Everything else is secondary to this need. This man has a really hard time saying no to his mother and often makes you take a back seat to her. He isn't really paying attention to what is going on with you because his need for approval from his parents is so strong that it takes most of his focus. He chooses work that will gain the approval of his parents. He doesn't pay a lot of attention to what your dreams and desires are because he needs to focus on his in order to receive his parents' approval.

The other side of Son Energy is Son Energy - Indifferent. A man in this energy is much like a woman in Daughter Energy. As a husband, he is the guy who is always watching "the game" and he believes that that is an important part of his life. He expects to be able to sit in front of the TV for hours at a time, whether it is watching a game or playing video games, and he expects you to take care of all of his needs, including all of his laundry and all of the cooking and cleaning. He has been raised to be "The Little Prince". He is narcissistic and believes that his needs are all that matter. He has tantrums when things don't go his way. He doesn't want you to pursue your dreams and desires because he is afraid you won't be around to take care of his needs. A man in Son Energy - Indifferent is indifferent to everything that is outside of himself. A man in Man Energy is none of these. He understands that his role is protector. He understands that it is his job to make you feel safe. He understands that when you feel safe, you can thrive. A man in Man Energy is present and engaged in his life. He doesn't check out by watching endless hours of sports or playing video games or hanging out endlessly with "the boys". He wants his wife to have and pursue her dreams and desires, for this makes her light up and she is more attractive to be around.

A man in Man Energy has an optimal balance of masculine and feminine energies. As I mentioned earlier, masculine energy is the structure or riverbank and feminine energy is the flow or river. A man in Man Energy has strong structure in the form of boundaries that support the greatest good of his family. A man in Father Energy typically has too much masculine energy and not enough feminine energy. He can either be very structured and rigid or is going at a frenetic pace. A man in Son Energy often has too much feminine energy and not enough masculine energy. His energy sort of spills all over the place without enough direction.

The natural essence of a man is to be in Man Energy. He is strong and confident and he always has your back. Men, in general, unless they are narcissistic, are wired to please women. It is built into their makeup to want to please women. We have to give them the space to do that.

Just as a woman in Woman Energy takes responsibility for all aspects of her life (but not responsibility for what is not hers to be responsible for), a man in Man Energy takes responsibility for his life. He doesn't blame everyone around him for what is wrong in his life and he doesn't fling his emotions all over the place. He sees himself as a valuable contributor to the well-being of his family and his household.

Perhaps your husband was in Man Energy when you first met and that was what was so attractive about him. As a woman in Mother Energy, to show him that you loved him, you started to do more for him, which gave him less space for him to do things for himself. You did his laundry; he didn't have to. You took out the garbage; he didn't have to. You organized everything and all things; he didn't have to. Now he is sitting back thinking, "You have taken all of this away from me because you think you can do it better than me, so do it." Unfortunately, as a woman in Mother Energy, you are now exhausted and filled with resentment and hostility and you wonder how your husband became so lazy when he didn't start out that way.

Perhaps your husband started out in Son Energy and you just expected that he was going to somehow wake up one day and decide he needed to be in Man Energy, all the while you were doing everything for him. Where is the space in the relationship for him to become this if you aren't requiring it through your actions and boundaries?

Maybe your husband started out in Father Energy and you felt that by doing everything for him, as a woman in Mother Energy does, that he would either soften and show appreciation once in a while or stop doing things for everyone else and pay more attention to you. Unfortunately, you have never required him to be different. You just keep doing everything for him. If you are in Daughter Energy and require everything to be done for you and to be taken care of, how is your husband going to be in Man Energy? He is more likely to be in Father Energy. He will either treat you like a child and have the final say or he will be run ragged trying to do everything to please you; all the while you are deeply dissatisfied. If your husband is in Son Energy, your needs will often not be met because your husband is demanding you take care of him and you are demanding he take care of you. Whoever is more demanding will "win".

Where do you start setting boundaries with your husband and how do you begin? Start paying attention to the issues that bother you and ask yourself. "Why does this bother me?" Also ask yourself, "How am I contributing to this?" and "What outcome do I want if I set a boundary in this area?" Remember, if you want your husband to move into Man Energy, you need to be willing to move into Woman Energy, meaning that you have to be willing to give up control of the issue if you are in Mother Energy and you have to be willing to step up and be responsible for things if you are in Daughter Energy. Otherwise, your husband has no space in which to operate.

Generally speaking, men are better at setting boundaries than women are. They are raised to believe that their time matters and their needs are important and they are given the space to pursue their dreams and desires. Pay attention to where your husband has boundaries. Realize as well that some of these boundaries are there by default – because you had no boundaries, something took shape for your husband. Where does your husband expect things to be a certain way? Do you desire these same things for yourself? Know that if he has the right to expect these, then you have the right to expect these. Does your husband schedule in playtime – golf, hockey, etc? This is one of his boundaries. It is scheduled in and he expects it to be respected. Do you have playtime scheduled in? Do you expect that time to be respected? If your husband can expect this, then so can you. Here are some questions to ask yourself to determine where you need some boundaries with your husband:

Can you buy clothing for yourself without asking for your husband's permission? Do you feel guilty if you do so?

If you bring a purchase home and your husband doesn't like it, do you feel you must return it?

Have you ever made a major purchase (such as a piece of fitness equipment or computer) without first running it by your husband? Does your husband make such decisions without discussing it with you first?

Does your husband feel he has the right to veto your decisions? Do you feel you have an equal right to veto his?

Are you always giving in to your husband's preferences for how to spend time and money?

If your husband makes more money than you do, does that automatically mean that his career is taken more seriously and is seen as more important than yours?

Have you deferred your career development needs for the sake of your husband's career or well-being?

Are you constantly on the receiving end of criticism or unsolicited advice from your husband about how you should live your life?

If you answered yes to some, most or all of these questions, you are holding beliefs that are undermining your well-being.

As you answered these questions did any of the following statements come to mind?

- The needs of others are more important than mine.
- My needs don't matter.
- It is selfish to take care of my needs first.
- I was raised to believe that taking care of others is what matters.
- I was raised to believe that my husband is more important than I am.
- My husband will only like me if I do everything he asks of me and expects from me.
- If my husband makes more money than I do, he is more important than I am.

- Saying no to a request is unacceptable.
- If I don't take care of this, no one will.

All of these beliefs are Mother Energy and Daughter Energy beliefs. A woman in Woman Energy wouldn't hold these beliefs. She may have when she started moving into Woman Energy but she has cleared them out to make way for the beliefs that support her so that she can set the boundaries she requires. She believes that she does matter; that her needs matter; that taking care of her needs first is compassionate, not only to herself, but also to the others around her; and that she has the right to say no to anything and everything.

My husband, Mark, and I have been married for over 23 years and we have been together for 29 years. For most of our marriage, I was strongly in Mother Energy and Mark was in Son Energy. Mark did little around the house for most of our marriage. He may have been interested in the beginning, but because I was so strongly in Mother Energy, there was no space for him to do something. I just did it all; that way it got done.

I have only been in Woman Energy for the last couple of years and not fully in it for that time. I have learned a lot from the process. I have learned that if I require Mark to do something, he is willing *but* it has to be on his time, not mine, and for Mark, that means when the clock hands align or the moon is full in the sky or whatever bizarre timing he feels is appropriate. In the past, I would simply have said, "Fine, don't bother. I will just do it myself." Now, I ask him to commit to when he is going to do the task. By asking Mark when he is going to do the task, he feels like he is in control instead of me controlling him. Getting Mark to pick a time requires his buy-in and commitment.

A woman in Woman Energy lets her husband know that if he doesn't do the task that he committed to doing, he is eroding her trust in him. She isn't telling him in some kind of manipulative way. She is simply informing him in a calm way that this is the outcome if he doesn't honor his commitment. This gives him the information he requires to maintain her trust. It also lets him know what the result will be if he doesn't do this. A man in Man Energy doesn't want to erode his wife's trust and he doesn't want to erode trust with himself.

Mark insisting on a time that worked for him taught me something really important. If my husband gets to establish the timing of an activity, then so do I. People generally think there needs to be compromise in relationships. Is compromise a good thing? Think about compromise. Does it have a good feeling to it? Does this leave you feeling less than? Compromise takes a piece of you away. It diminishes you. A compromise is not a healthy choice because you are not choosing this option. You are being forced into this option. It makes you feel like you are giving up a piece of yourself.

Concessions, on the other hand are healthy responses to a situation. Feel how the word concession feels. It feels open. It feels like you have a choice. Are you open to this option? Are you receptive to this option? Do you feel content after accepting this option? Do you feel you are still whole? Do you feel heard? Concessions are healthy and powerful as long as you aren't the only person in the relationship that is constantly making concessions. If this is the case, then you are settling – settling for less than you deserve, less than you desire.

Mark used to demand that I drop whatever I was doing to attend to his wants and needs. I constantly put my needs aside to attend to his. A few months back, I was getting ready for a tele-seminar that I was attending and I was starting to run a bit behind with getting ready. I was starting to move a bit faster to be ready on time. Mark knew that I was getting ready for the tele-seminar, which was starting soon. Mark, who is an architect, was playing around on his computer with one of his house designs. This was a design for himself and not for a client. In the middle of my rush to get ready, Mark asked that I stop what I was doing to give him an opinion on his design. I stopped what I was doing – an automatic response for a woman in Mother Energy - and started to look at Mark's design, which was a compromise for me.

The light bulb went off in my head. If my husband had the right to establish his timing for attending to what I required him to do, then I had the same right to establish my timing to attend to what he required. I stopped looking at his design and said, "You know I am getting ready for my tele-seminar and you know that it starts in a few minutes. If I continue to help you right now, I will miss the start of the seminar. When the seminar is finished, I will help you out." Mark initially started to have a tantrum. I simply explained to him that just as he had the right to set boundaries around his time, so did I also have that right. There was nothing Mark could say to that. He knew that that was true. End of discussion.

This scenario has happened a few more times since but Mark is learning that my time matters because I have decided that it matters and that I have the right and requirement to establish timing and timeframes that support me. If Mark has a request for my attention, I will let him know when I will be able to attend to it. By me establishing a boundary around my time, Mark was required to make a concession instead of me having to compromise. This was supportive for both of us. All of that being said, if something was really urgent, I would require Mark to take care of it right away and I would do the same for Mark if he had something that was urgent.

Are you saying yes to something just to make or keep your husband (or anyone else for that matter) happy even though this really doesn't work for you? If so, you are compromising. Had I said yes to Mark's demand, I would have compromised what was important to and for me.

As I have moved into Woman Energy fully and provided space for Mark to step up, he has chosen to do so with ease. I can see how important it has been for him to be given the space and opportunity to do things around the house, whether it is putting the groceries away, paying some of the bills, doing the laundry or whatever. I can see his sense of pride in himself for doing these tasks and I can feel his sense of joy in knowing that he is pleasing me. Mark does very little in the same way that I do things. He folds towels differently. He puts the food on different shelves in the pantry. He puts socks together differently. Does it really matter? No. Was this hard for me in the beginning? Absolutely. Are these tasks getting done without me having to do them? Absolutely. Would I rather do these tasks myself? Absolutely not. By letting go of my need for everything to be done my way, it has become a win-win situation for both of us. I have more time and energy to pursue my dreams and desires and Mark is excited to be an active participant in our household instead of merely an observer. As I let go of some of the structure, there is more flow in my life. Things are easier for both of us. We are both starting to thrive.

Establishing boundaries with your husband is really a retraining process. It won't happen overnight and it takes consistency on your part to make it so. Honor yourself enough to stick with it. Require your husband to respect you because you respect yourself and require your husband to respect your time because you respect your time. You need to show him that you value and respect yourself, you value and respect your time, you value and respect your needs and wants, and you require all of these to be valued and respected by him. You teach people how to treat you.

Take these learnings with your husband and extend them to other areas of your life. Does your manager or co-worker (male or female) believe that his or her time matters but yours doesn't? Do your older children believe that their needs are crucial but yours aren't? Does your mother believe that you need to be at her beck and call, but she isn't available for you? If their time matters then your time matters. If their needs are crucial, then your needs are crucial. If they aren't available for you, then you don't need to be available for them.

Boundaries and Gifts

I wanted to write a brief section on boundaries and gifts and I am including it here because this seems to be a difficult area between husbands and wives. I will use Christmas as the example because it is the biggest gift-giving occasion of the year. The principles of this apply whether you celebrate Christmas or not and they apply to all gift-giving occasions.

Do you remember when you were a little girl at Christmas and you put together a list for Santa of what you wanted? Do you remember how specific you were? There was nothing vague about your desires and you certainly didn't expect Santa to guess what you wanted. Why is it now, as a grown woman, you expect your husband (or friends or other family members) to guess what is on your mind and what your desires are? I often hear women say, "If he was paying attention, he would know what I want." Or, "If he loved me, he would know what will make me happy." How is he supposed to know? This behavior is a recipe for great heartache for both of you (or your friend or other family members).

This is a terribly selfish way to be and this is really a Daughter Energy behavior, whether you are in Daughter Energy or Mother Energy. More importantly, you are giving your responsibility for your desires to someone else. You are expecting someone else to figure out what you desire. As a woman in Woman Energy, your responsibilities are your responsibility. You are responsible for your desires, whether they are your soul dreams and desires or your gift wish list.

A lot of women push this wish list onto their husbands because they have no idea what they desire and they make their husbands responsible for figuring this out. If you abdicate this responsibility to your husband (or friend or other family members), you have no right to be upset if you end up receiving wiper blades and a gift card from the gas station as your Christmas gift. You are responsible for figuring your desires out. This is part of your operating instructions.

If you can't take the time to figure out what you desire to receive in the form of a gift, why should your husband (or friend or other family members) take the time to go out and guess what you would like? Your spouse may or may not be interested in putting in the time to run around and guess what you desire. He may have put in the time in the past only to have you express disappointment with the gift(s) he gave you. It is quite crushing for people to put time into a gift buying guessing game only to have their efforts shot down.

A simple way to resolve this is to take responsibility for what you desire. Take some time to figure this out. If you are too busy for this step, you need to rearrange your life so that you have some time for yourself. This is a symptom of a bigger problem in your life. Next, put together a wish list with options on it for your husband (or friend or other family members) to choose from. If you only desire one item, put this one item on your list. If you would like to receive things in a descending order of desire, list your priorities at the top and list the items in the order of your preferences. If you are equally excited about all of the items on your list, let the giver know that all items are equal in desire for you. If you really want diamond earrings, put this on your list. If this desire goes beyond the budget you have set, be grown up enough to not put this on your list. Gift giving isn't about causing financial harm.

If your husband is selfish and isn't interested in gifting you anything, know that this behavior has nothing to do with you. You are worthy of receiving gifts. In this case, it is important that you gift something to yourself. Although it won't be a surprise, you are honoring yourself by doing this.

14

Your Boundaries and the Digital World

What kind of boundaries do you have for your electronic devices and the digital world? Do you have any boundaries around these? Have you given any of this any thought? Are you on your devices (smart phone, tablet, etc) all of the time? Do you constantly check them while at work? Do you check them while in the middle of conversations with friends? Do you check them at dinner? Do you leave them on throughout the night? Can anyone get a hold of you at any time of the day or night?

Do you have limits for your children? Do you require dinner to be device-free? Do you require your children to turn off their devices at a certain time each day? Do you enforce these limits? Do you take your children's devices away from them each night at a designated time? Do you check your children's devices for their activities to make sure that they aren't inviting trouble?

If anyone and everyone has full access to you day and night ask yourself, "Why does everyone and anyone need access to me at all hours of the day and night?" Are you beholden to them? Are you afraid you will miss out on something? Do you believe it is the polite thing to do? Do you truly want to be in constant contact with everyone and anyone? Does this feel intrusive to you? Does it satisfy a need you have to be needed? Does all of this interaction please you? Does it please you to interact with everyone that you interact with? Are there people you need to interact with a lot less? Why aren't you allowing yourself to limit this interaction?

What if you set limits on when you answer people's correspondence (texts, calls, emails, Facebook updates, tweets)? How would this make you feel? Would you feel selfish for not getting back to people right away? If you placed limits on this access and your correspondence, and this freed up some time, what would you rather be doing? How would having some time available during your day make you feel?

What about your phone and your children? I see so many women talking on their phones while their children drag behind them. Often the children are struggling to find ways to get their mom's attention. I have heard many kids say, "Mom put your phone away. Stop talking on your phone." Are your children such a drag that you would rather have a conversation on the phone than with them? You are sending your children a very dangerous message – they don't matter.

Do you feel it is selfish or rude if someone calls your phone and you don't answer it? Do you feel you are being unselfish by always answering your phone when it rings? What if you were in the middle of something – dinner, a transaction at the store, a conversation with the person you are with? How is it unselfish and not rude to answer your phone in the middle of these activities but selfish to not answer the call that is interrupting you? Is it possible that your phone is for your convenience and not for the convenience of the person calling or texting you? Is it possible that not answering every call as your phone is ringing and not responding to every text right away would actually help you feel less frazzled and calmer? Would you be okay with that? Would you be less stressed if you simply drove your vehicle without having a phone conversation? Are the majority of your conversations, texts, tweets, Facebook updates and the like pressing and urgent? Are they necessary? Are they adding to the pleasure in your life or taking away the pleasure in your life?

Do you like being "on-call"? When people are on-call for work purposes, they get paid for being available and ready to take work-related action for a specified period of time. When you are on-call in your private life, you are giving this time away for free without receiving any form of compensation for your availability. How does that make you feel? Do you feel resentment around being always available? Do you feel like your life is always being intruded upon? How does it feel to be available to all people all of the time? Does this make you feel happy? Enlivened? Constricted? Exhausted? Overwhelmed? Taken advantage of? Needed? Useful? Helpful?

What about Facebook, Twitter, Instagram and whatever other social media sites you are on? Do you have boundaries around these? Do you limit who you are "friends" with? Do these people make you feel better about yourself? Do they make you feel worse about yourself? Does your interaction on these sites make your life feel expanded or constricted? Do you feel anxious because you aren't sure if you will have something to say that everyone will applaud you for? Do you find that instead of actually living your life you spend your time trying to look like you are living your life in a way that appeals to your audience? Does this make you feel better about yourself? Do you feel authentic?

Do you find your friends' comments often upset you? Why would you want interlopers commenting on how you live? Why do you need people to comment on how you live? Does this make you feel better about yourself or worse? Do you need their approval? What if they don't approve?

Do you constantly suffer from anxiety? Are you constantly afraid you are missing out? Are you suffering from an addiction to these sites and activities? Could you cut them out of your life completely tomorrow? How much time are these sites and your involvement with them sucking out of your life? How many hours a day do you spend on Facebook, Twitter, Instagram and the like? What else could you do with this time? Could you be more present with your kids? With your spouse? Would you be more present at work and get more done in an easier manner?

If you can't or won't give up these sites and activities, can you put limits on your activity? What if you gave yourself one hour a day to catch up on these sites? Would this make you feel stressed? Liberated? What if you restricted the number of "friends" and kept the people who make you feel better about yourself and who want the best for you and got rid of everyone else from these sites that made you feel worse about yourself and who don't want the best for you? Would that be possible? Would this be selfish or self-full? If you feel this is selfish, ask yourself why. Why is protecting yourself from social parasites selfish? Why do you feel and believe that you don't have the right to protect yourself from harm? Do you feel that this limitation would hurt the feelings of those you are freeing yourself from? Do these people worry about hurting your feelings with all of the comments they post and tweet? Takers are never concerned with your feelings. You need to know that you have the right to protect your feelings by freeing yourself of harmful people. You need to help your children do the same.

Does everyone in your family need to know what you are up to? Could you block out intrusive family members? Do you believe that you have that right? It is important for you to know that you do, indeed, have the right to block out any intrusive person from your digital experience. It is imperative for your own well-being that you do so.

A woman in Woman Energy doesn't waste endless hours on Facebook, Twitter, Instagram and the like. She understands that these sites have a purpose, but she doesn't give them her every waking moment. She understands that she needs to be very protective of her time, so she uses it to her best advantage. She also understands that she feels a whole lot better about herself when she has interactions on these sites with people who lift her up and eliminates all interactions with people who drag her down. She has boundaries around when and with whom she responds. She doesn't give everyone in the world access to her and she shuts her devices off every evening.

15

Do You Have the Right to Pursue Your Dreams and Desires?

As women, we often struggle with the belief that it is selfish to pursue our own dreams and desires. A woman in Mother Energy has no time or space to pursue her dreams and desires and has likely forgotten what they are. A woman in Daughter Energy often doesn't feel capable of pursuing her dreams and desires or she expects others to make them happen for her. Your dreams and desires are the longing of your soul. Why do you suppose we have these longings if we weren't meant to pursue them?

A woman in Woman Energy understands that to live a fulfilling life she is required to pursue her dreams and desires. This requirement is part of your internal operating instructions for *you*. Boundaries around these are essential for these dreams and desires to become a reality.

Society tells us, as women, that we are supposed to desire becoming a mother and that desire is sufficient for us. Even if you believe that your soul's desire and purpose is to be a mother, it isn't your only desire and purpose. Your purpose and reason for being here on earth aren't supposed to end when your children leave home. That doesn't make any sense. According to Sanaya Roman, author of *Living With Joy*, your true purpose for being here on earth is to experience joy. If being a mother is part of that experience, great. If not being a mother is part of that experience, that's great as well.

Often pursuing our desires and dreams is a matter of timing. For example, if you desire to have a baby and start a business or pursue a degree or travel the world or whatever your heart is calling you to do, it is difficult to have both desires be born at the same time. Both require a lot of focus, energy, time and attention units and if you give birth to both at the same time, one or both of them will suffer. This doesn't mean, however, that because you have one you can't have the other. It also doesn't mean that you have to give up on the other.

When I was in my second year of university, I met a woman named Jill. We became friends. I was 20 and Jill was 32. It makes me laugh now but at the time, I thought Jill was old and quite frankly, I had never had someone so old in any of my classes. Jill clearly understood the principle of being required to pursue her dreams and desires. She came from a fairly conservative, religious upbringing and she got married when she was 20. Jill knew that she was expected to have a family and she also desired that. When I met her, Jill had four children, ranging in ages from 11 to 4. As much as being a mother filled Jill up, she also had a deep, burning desire to get her university degree. She knew that this desire would be accomplished, but in the right time. Her children were at a point in their lives that allowed Jill to pursue her deep desire of getting a degree. Jill was remarkable. She had very strong boundaries around all of this. There wasn't anything that would stop her from fulfilling her dream. Jill had each day mapped out. She had her classes scheduled for when her children were at school or daycare. She had "children time" scheduled in and she had study time scheduled in. She got her children to bed at an early time in the evening, both so that they would be their best in the morning but also so that Jill would have the time necessary to devote to her studying. Jill had buy-in from her husband, who was strongly in Man Energy and understood how important this dream was to Jill and wanted to do what he could to make it happen.

I marveled at Jill. At 20 years old, I couldn't imagine what it took for her to make all of this happen, not because I didn't think that I could do remarkable things myself but because of my socially ingrained notion that said that being a mother was all-consuming and that there wasn't space in a mother's life for pursuing a degree. This notion, in itself, was strange because my mom worked one, two and sometimes three jobs and she still had the time and space for me and my sisters and all of our activities (although I really have no idea how she did it).

Just to be clear here, Jill wasn't Superwoman nor did she see herself that way. She was strongly in Woman Energy and she had a burning desire to fulfill. She established strong boundaries with everyone with whom she needed boundaries – her children, her husband, her parents, and her friends. She expected these boundaries to be respected. She expected her dream to be respected. Jill knew that pursuing her desire of getting her degree was really important for her soul and that pursuing this desire showed her daughters that this was a critical component of living a fulfilled life. Jill did not allow herself to mess around in the guilt space. She had a strict boundary around this as well. For Jill, pursuing this desire of getting her degree was God-directed. She had a deep knowing that living a life that lit her up gave other women permission to live that way as well. Jill felt that this showed the goodness of God in her life – showing people the way to a fulfilled life.

My mom, on the other hand, chose the opposite for herself. My mom had always wanted to be a nurse but never became one. I never knew if it was because she didn't believe she could do it or for some other reason. She always regretted not becoming a nurse and she always had a strong resentment energy around this.

I learned a couple of things from this. First, you never want to have regret about something. Regret is a very heavy energy that is difficult to disentangle from and requires a lot of forgiveness of yourself – something a lot of women aren't willing to do. You always walk around wondering what it would have been like if you pursued your desire.

The second thing I learned from this is that if you are not pursuing your desires and what is in your heart, you will always believe that everyone else needs to somehow pay for this. I don't think women understand that when we deny ourselves the opportunity to pursue our desires we become filled with resentment, which we believe everyone else is supposed to somehow make up for. It is an enormous burden for your children to feel they have to somehow make up for your lost dreams. You have probably never thought about your desires this way but think about it. Do you really want your children to be burdened with the weight of your unfulfilled dreams and desires? Wouldn't it simply be healthier for all involved for you to pursue what is in your heart?

This is not all or nothing. It is not like you are to pursue what is calling you in your heart to the exclusion of all else in your life. Everything requires balance. Balance requires boundaries. A woman in Woman Energy understands this.

A key understanding to pursuing your dreams and desires is having your biochemistry in alignment with this. Most women do not understand what this means and therefore do not use their biochemistry to work in their favor, which would allow them to receive their desires more readily. In order to pursue and receive your dreams and desires you need to be in an oxytocin state. As women, we do not thrive with adrenaline flowing through our bodies. Men actually do thrive with adrenaline running through their bodies, which is why motivational seminars and motivational speakers work really well for men. When men get "pumped up" with adrenaline, they are ready to "go to battle". Men's bodies are designed to be in a sympathetic state meaning that they are wired to have their sympathetic nervous systems awake and turned on. The sympathetic nervous system is responsible for priming the body for action and for the fight or flight response.

As women, on the other hand, we are designed to have our parasympathetic nervous systems awake and turned on. The parasympathetic nervous system is responsible for rest and digest activities. Oxytocin activates the parasympathetic nervous system. When we, as women, are in an oxytocin state we are in a tend and befriend state, which means that we feel an internal state of safety where we are connected to ourselves. This state is important for being grounded and fulfilled as a woman. Oxytocin allows us to connect and collaborate, both with our desires and with others. It allows us to trust ourselves and trust our desires.

Our bodies become addicted to the neurochemicals that are constantly released. Negative thinking increases the release of cortisol, which keeps our addicted brain and body happy. This means that we need to keep thinking or finding negative thoughts in order to increase our cortisol levels. If you are addicted to adrenaline, you often create "back against the wall" types of scenarios in order to increase the release of adrenaline. Neither of these states help you move forward towards your desires.

The moment our bodies get the "I need to survive" message from our thinking and mental field, the fight or flight response kicks in and our bodies release adrenaline. We then start thinking, "What's in it for me? It's too late. It's too much. I'm not even sure it is possible. I'm not worth it. I can't do it. What's the point? It will never happen for me." The adrenaline state causes our metabolism to diminish and our vitality to decrease. Energy is taken away from our organs and the glow of our skin diminishes. We start to feel fatigued and then we start to feel doubt. Now we are in a state of flight and we energetically flee our bodies and we check out. Layers of doubt cover over our enthusiasm and we give up.

Only when we feel safe and are in our bodies do we have the biochemistry to thrive. We need to retrain our bodies to feel safe. When we feel safe, we don't go into the "what ifs". When we feel safe, we feel eager for our desires to unfold. Eagerness is a thriving emotion. Excitement, on the other hand, is an adrenaline emotion. When we feel excitement, we start to feel attachment. When we feel attachment to an outcome or person, we tap into the fear of abandonment. Abandonment is a basic element of survival.

As mentioned earlier, a woman in Woman Energy is in an oxytocin state. She understands the requirement for this and ensures that this is the biochemistry she is experiencing. A woman in Woman Energy also understands that pursuing her dreams and desires is purely for the journey, for the joy of mastery. She is not pursuing these desires for the outcomes they may bring for this is attachment energy which, as mentioned, is an adrenaline state. A woman in Woman Energy understands that mastery is a state of becoming. It takes roughly 10,000 hours for us to develop a skill or activity to the point where we have mastery or unconscious competence with it. This means that the skill or activity can be performed by the subconscious mind at the level of competence.

When you remember this, you don't go into fight or flight. When you pursue your dreams and desires in the energy of a student, you are grounded and people will feel this. When you respect this law, your body will go from the sympathetic state to the parasympathetic state.

When you are in the parasympathetic or oxytocin state, you become an influencer. An influencer is someone who is so connected to her sense of inspiration that she can influence others to connect to their own inspiration. When you are in oxytocin, others feel a sense of trust with you. You are able to respond rather than react to the situation. This helps you become more powerful within and this allows for collaboration. When you are in an adrenaline state, you feel unsafe and others feel you as unsafe. This adrenaline state makes you react to the situation and it makes it impossible for you to respond to the situation. Reacting makes you bitchy and makes others perceive you as a bitch. This brings out competition, which makes it virtually impossible for you to move your desires forward.

A woman in Woman Energy understands there is no healthy competition for women, except if they are in competitive sports, and that being and remaining in an oxytocin state is essential for her to move her dreams and desires forward.

Just exactly how do you get into an oxytocin state? First, decide that is how you want to live your life. If you believe it is impossible to live your life that way, know that it is true. Whatever you believe – is true for you. If you believe that it is possible to live your life this way, know that it is true. When I first learned this information, I was so past the point of being overwhelmed and exhausted that I was simply excited to know there was a better, healthier, more peaceful way to live.

Second, you need to be retraining your body to release oxytocin instead of adrenaline. This is a boundary issue and is part of your internal operating instructions.

Focusing on bringing pleasure into your life will help to retrain your brain and your body to release oxytocin. Pleasure is an oxytocin state. Using better, higher vibrating words will help retrain your brain and body to release oxytocin. For example, when you say, "I am excited ..." or "I need ..." or "I am anxious to ..." or "When is it going to happen?" these put you into an adrenaline state. I also find the word "deadline" to be an adrenaline word. Just the thought of it makes me feel anxious. For me, a better phrase is "action point" because a deadline is usually a point in time that someone else needs to take action on whatever it is that you are working on. When you say, "I am enthusiastic ..." or "I trust ..." or "I am eager to ..." or "I feel safe that this is coming" these statements put you in an oxytocin state.

In addition to words, different emotions cause you to release adrenaline or oxytocin. When you feel emotions such as worry, embarrassment, disappointment, rejection, guilt, jealousy, drama or resentment you are in an adrenaline state. When you feel emotions of inspiration, courage, hope, trust, joy and love you are in an oxytocin state. Your words and your emotions are all boundary issues. These are part of your internal operating instructions. Choose to have a boundary around your words and your emotions.

Additional ways to increase oxytocin are through different forms of touch. Hugging is an excellent way to increase oxytocin. Have at least one hug a day with someone you love and trust. This hug should last for at least 10 seconds. Receive a massage by someone you trust. Massage is great way to increase oxytocin. It is also a great way to become grounded. Being grounded and in your body releases oxytocin. When you are up in your head, you are not grounded, you are not present and you are in an adrenaline state. Oxytocin is released during orgasm, so having sex with someone you love and trust is a great way to increase oxytocin.

A final suggestion for increasing oxytocin is through your breath. Inhaling activates the sympathetic nervous system and exhaling activates the parasympathetic nervous system. If you make a pleasurable sound out loud when you exhale slowly, you will activate the release of oxytocin. Allow the inhale to fill your belly then exhale slowly making a pleasurable sound. Do several of these breaths in a row and do them several times a day. This will help retrain your brain and your body to release oxytocin. When you are in an oxytocin state, you are ready to move your dreams and desires forward and in a pleasurable way.

I often hear women say that they have no idea what their dreams and desires are. Women often feel so defeated for not even knowing what these are. It has either been so long since they gave their dreams and desires any thought that they have no idea what they are or they are so busy that there isn't any clarity around what they are. Sometimes, though, women pretend that they don't know what their dreams and desires are because they understand at a deep level that these dreams and desires are big – too big – for them to handle so they hide out in confusion and lack of clarity. These women are afraid that if they pursued their big dreams and big desires everyone would abandon them and they would be left all alone. Abandonment is a basic element of survival and it activates adrenaline. So, these women hide out in adrenaline claiming that they feel safer there than in the energy of their dreams and desires. They need to understand that they wouldn't have these big dreams and desires in their heart if they weren't meant to pursue them. Much of this fear is subconscious programming and cellular memories, both of which need to be released. Releasing all of this "mind junk" will enable these women to move their dreams and desires forward.

Sometimes, though, women simply lack clarity around what their heart is calling them to do. What we, as women, generally don't know is that while we are running around in adrenaline, we won't and can't have any clarity. Adrenaline blocks clarity. So, until we get into an oxytocin state, we will not have a clear understanding of what our dreams and desires are. It should give you comfort to know that your lack of clarity isn't because you don't care about your dreams and desires or that the time for them has passed. Moving into oxytocin and out of adrenaline will help you gain clarity. It will also help you gain enthusiasm for your dreams and desires and will help you feel more confident that your dreams and desires are possible.

A woman in Woman Energy understands that we have a set amount of attention units each week. Attention units can be thought of as units of mental energy available to us to attend to what needs to be attended to and with which to make decisions. A woman in Woman Energy understands that we have more units available at the beginning of the week and that by the time we have made "a million decisions" we have few units remaining at the end of the week. This means that a woman in Woman Energy, as best as she can, schedules important meetings and appointments for the beginning of the week and schedules playtime at the end of the week. She understands that to move her dreams and desires forward, she doesn't waste attention units frivolously on Facebook, Twitter, Instagram and the like. She also understands that to move her dreams and desires forward, she must give them some attention units each week, even if the timing isn't right for them to be born now. She also doesn't waste attention units with pointless worry.

As well, a woman in Woman Energy understands that the set amount of attention units gets used up easily through decision making. So, instead of using up her units making decisions all week long for everyone in her life, she allows and requires everyone in her life to make age-appropriate decisions. A woman in Woman Energy doesn't join committees that she has no interest in joining for she knows that these committees will take up attention units that would be better served in a different way.

And, because a woman in Woman Energy understands how important attention units are and how they get used up, she focuses on being grounded in her body so that her energy is not all up in her head being consumed with endless thinking and mind chatter. To be grounded in her body, she focuses on bringing her energy out of her head and down into her belly, about four fingers below her belly button. A woman in Woman Energy understands that this is where her power comes from and she focuses on keeping her energy there. By having energy in her lower belly and not up in her head, she is now able to be present. This means she can attend to what she needs to attend to with greater ease. Being present also means that this woman's life is not being run by her subconscious mind.

According to Dr. Bruce Lipton, author of *The Honeymoon Effect – The Science of Creating Heaven on Earth*, the conscious mind is your creative mind and is the source of your dreams and desires. The moment you start thinking, you are no longer in your conscious mind. You are now operating from your subconscious mind. Your subconscious mind contains all of your default programming, which is the patterning and behaviors of other people, and the desires and dreams of other people – your parents, your teachers, and anyone who had influence over you when you were young.

At this point, you are running the same patterns and behaviors as your parents, etc, and you are running their dreams and desires. Your subconscious mind does not contain your dreams and desires. It contains other people's dreams and desires. You need to be in your conscious mind where your dreams and desires are contained in order for you to pursue your dreams and desires.

This is a really critical point so I will say it again. You need to be in your conscious mind in order for you to pursue your dreams and desires.

According to Dr. Lipton, a typical day looks like this - ninety-five percent of the day our mind is thinking which means that for 95 percent of our day we run programs that contain other people's beliefs and behaviors. Seventy percent of these programs are negative and self-sabotaging. What all of this means is that we spend 95 percent of our day not in our dreams and desires. No wonder it is so hard for us to pursue our dreams and desires. If you stay mindful and present, you are in your conscious mind and you are able to manifest your dreams and desires.

Our identity of who we think we are is actually who other people tell us we are, which includes the beliefs that we don't deserve this and/or we aren't lovable. Most of our subconscious programming is actually criticism by others and is programmed into us. If "I don't deserve..." is programmed into your subconscious mind, your behaviors will create situations and outcomes that "prove" you don't deserve it. To create your dreams and desires, you need to operate from your creative mind, your conscious mind. You do this by being mindful and being in the present and by changing the subconscious programming you have going on.

All of the above are part of a Woman Energy woman's internal operating instructions for herself. A woman in Woman Energy understands that it is up to her to pursue her dreams and desires and that she has the responsibility both to not let them slide away and clear out whatever subconscious programming is in the way.

SECTION FOUR

Becoming Woman Energy™ and Stepping Into the Master Boundary

16

How Do You Become Woman Energy™?

So it is all good and fine to decide you want to be in Woman Energy but how do you go about becoming that when your lifelong pattern has been to be in anything but that energy? How do you actually "be" in Woman Energy in a way that you remain there easily?

On one hand, stepping into Woman Energy is simple. We simply are that energy, if we choose to be. This is our natural essence as women. We are born with this knowing. We simply have been conditioned out of this natural essence. Once you have decided to be in that energy you will notice that you will start to become that energy.

The challenge, however, is that we have lots of energy blocking us and this energy needs to be shifted in order for us to become our radiant, powerful Woman Energy selves. I will cover more on shifting this energy in the next chapter.

You have lifelong patterns of being in energy other than Woman Energy, so you need to pay attention to how you are being as you go throughout your day. As you pay attention to the people, activities and interactions that are trying to pull you out of Woman Energy and back into whatever dominant archetype you were in before, you will have the opportunity to choose to stay centered and grounded in Woman Energy or allow yourself to be pulled back into your old patterns.

As with any change you desire to make, the first step is to decide that you are ready to make the change. If you are not ready to make the change, nothing will happen. So, to be in Woman Energy, you need to decide that this is what you desire and that you are really ready to give up the other patterns you have been employing.

The next step is to allow yourself to get clear on your WHY. Why are you now ready? Why do you desire now to be in Woman Energy? Your WHY will provide you with the power to continue with this process. If you don't have a strong WHY, you simply have a wish. This wish won't give you the strength to make this change happen. As you move into Woman Energy, some people and perhaps lots of people will provide some or a lot of resistance as you make this change. These people will protest your desire to live your life in a way that lifts you up. If you aren't clear with your WHY, these people will persuade you to remain as you have always been. It serves them. If your WHY is crystal clear to you, nothing will stop you from becoming a woman who lives in Woman Energy.

An example of a strong WHY is: "Moving into and staying in Woman Energy will allow me to become the woman that I truly am and allow me to pursue desires that light me up as a woman. I know that there is a better, easier, more fulfilling way to live my life. I know I am here to contribute my unique talents and abilities and being in Woman Energy will provide the platform for this to happen for me."

You can feel the energy in this. It feels expansive and optimistic.

An example of a weak WHY is: "My spouse or partner is tired of me always helping everyone. He/she wants all of my time and attention." With this as your WHY, you won't make the change.

Your WHY has to be about you and your desire for change. It can't be about someone else's desire for you to change. Changing for someone else will only build up more resentment in you. You will feel angry and resentful with no desire or energy to change.

This brings up an important point. Setting boundaries is solely for you. It isn't so that you can demand change from others. Demanding change from others only leads to anger and resentment in and from them just as it does for you when someone demands you change for them.

Once you have made the decision to move into Woman Energy and out of either Mother Energy or Daughter Energy and you have a strong WHY, you are ready to ask yourself a series of questions that will help you identify whether you are about to step outside of your Woman Energy circle and back into your old pattern. There is a series of questions for each of the four archetypes.

If your pattern is Mother Energy - Taken Advantage of, the point of being in Woman Energy is to get your life back for good. In order to do that, you need to know there are very few scenarios that would require you to say yes. Here are questions to ask yourself to help you identify if you are about to step outside of your Woman Energy circle.

Regarding the request, expectation, interaction or experience you are currently evaluating, ask:

1. Does this request, expectation, interaction or experience make me feel taken advantage of? Resentful? Hostile?

   If this makes you feel taken advantage of, ask, "What causes me to feel taken advantage of? Is it time to say no because I have allowed myself to be taken advantage of in the past?" Saying no keeps you in Woman Energy.

   If it makes you feel resentful, ask, "Why would I want to do something that makes me feel resentful?" Saying no to something that makes you feel resentful keeps you in Woman Energy.

   If it makes you feel hostile, ask, "Why would I want to do something that makes me feel hostile?" Saying no to something that makes you feel hostile keeps you in Woman Energy.

2. Is this the first time this person has asked for this? Yes or No?

   If yes, is the relationship or experience important to you? Yes or No?

   If the relationship or experience is important to you, do you have any interest in fulfilling the request or expectation or interaction or experience? If yes, are you trying to prove something? If you are trying to prove something, say no to the request or expectation or interaction or experience. You have nothing to prove. Be honest with yourself. You are honoring yourself by saying no. This helps to keep the energy in your relationship clean because you won't be filled with resentment and hostility. It also gives the other person the opportunity to be resourceful and have their requirement fulfilled in some other way. This keeps you in Woman Energy.

If the relationship or experience isn't important to you, say, no – end of discussion. This keeps you in Woman Energy.

If it isn't the first time the person has asked for this, unless it is a small child asking, say no. This will require the person to find a different way to get this done and it won't be on your shoulders. This keeps you in Woman Energy.

3. Will fulfilling this request or expectation cause you to be depleted? If yes, say no to the request or expectation. Women in Woman Energy do not allow themselves to become depleted. If it won't cause you to become depleted, do you have any interest in doing this? If yes, tell the person that you will need a day to think about it and you will get back to them. If you still feel interested in doing it a day from now, feel free to say yes.

If you won't feel depleted from doing this but you have no interest in doing it, say no. Enough said.

4. Will the request or expectation cause you to drop into force energy to get it done? If so, then definitely say no. Force energy drops you into adrenaline which will cause you to feel depleted, defeated and bitchy. This would take you out of Woman Energy.

   If you can fulfill the request without dropping into force energy, are you interested in doing it? If yes, tell the person that you will need a day to think about it and you will get back to them. If you still feel interested in doing it a day from now, feel free to say yes.

   If you won't drop into force energy from doing this but you have no interest in doing it, say no. Nothing more is required.

5. Is it something that will enhance your pleasure? If yes, do it. If no, don't do it.

6. Is this an opportunity for you to grow? If yes, feel free to say yes as long as it won't deplete you or cause you to drop into force energy. If it isn't an opportunity for you to grow, say no. You don't need more work. Either of these answers will keep you in Woman Energy.

7. Will it require you to organize something? Is this your comfort zone? Say no. You spend too much time organizing.

8. Will it give you the opportunity to do something totally differently and in more flow than you

would have done in the past? If so, feel free to say yes to this if you have the time, the energy, the interest, it won't deplete you and you won't drop back into force energy. If you can meet all of these requirements, you will stay in Woman Energy. If you can't meet all of these requirements, say no. This too, will keep you in Woman Energy.

Pay attention to what came up for you as you asked these questions. Awareness precedes a shift. Did you have thoughts like, "I don't have the right to say no. Who am I to require someone to find a different way of getting this done? What will people think of me if I say no? I am being selfish if I say no. Who do you think you are, saying no?"

All of these thoughts are part of your subconscious programming. They need to be changed and they can be changed so that you can ask the questions at the beginning and say a resounding no with ease, confidence and grace. Know that in doing so you are getting your life back. Stick with this.

If you are in Mother Energy - Taken Advantage of and you are moving into Woman Energy and doing less for everyone, the people who have expected and demanded that you do things for them and carry them are going to fight back. They are going to be angry that you are no longer carrying them. They will tell you that you are being selfish for making these changes. They will tell you that they feel you no longer care about them. They will make you feel bad about yourself. Don't give in to this. These people need to start taking care of themselves and carrying their own purses.

As you start to feel like you can breathe again, finally, and you have some time and space for yourself, allow yourself to feel how good this feels. Let these people know that you still care about them, if that is your truth, and let them know that you need to continue to require them to carry their own purses. Allowing and requiring them to take care of themselves while you take care of yourself for the first time in a long time, if ever, will feel very liberating and powerful. Relish this. Allow this feeling of expansion and freedom to be your guide when the takers demand you get back to the way things were. Their tantrums will continue for a bit. Don't give in to them. Eventually these takers will take care of their own requirements and needs or they will find someone else to do it for them.

As you stand firm and continue to move into Woman Energy, it will become apparent to the people around these takers that it has been you who has made them look good at work or on the committee or wherever you have been carrying them. If you have been carrying your children who are old enough to carry themselves, it is time to stop. Your children need to step up. This will benefit them enormously. They will start to turn on their own capabilities and discover their own greatness. If you have been carrying your colleague at work and you are no longer willing to do so, his or her lack of effort or skill/knowledge will start to show up for others to finally see. All of the accolades your colleague received while you carried him or her will no longer be given.

Your brilliance will start to shine. As you start to focus on doing just your own job, you will have more energy available to apply to your own work. As you move into Woman Energy and out of Mother Energy - Taken Advantage of, you will feel a lot less resentment and more contentment and even happiness. This is reason enough to push through the resistance of the takers.

If you are in Mother Energy - Intrusive, there are very few occasions where you would need to say yes to the questions below because most of your activity has been uninvited to this point. The people you have helped in the past either didn't want or ask for it *or* they simply expected you to keep bailing them out without being interested in changing for the better. The point of being in Woman Energy for you is so that you can focus on your own life. Ask yourself these questions:

1. Did the person I am about to help ask for my help? Yes or No?

    If no, stop yourself from jumping in to help this person. This person doesn't want or require your help and may have simply been sharing what was going on in his or her life. Or, this person needs to be responsible to figure this situation out on his or her own. Even if this person is a younger child, give him or her the space to come up with options. Then you can help this person understand what the outcome of each option could be. This will keep you in Woman Energy.

    If the person did ask for help, ask yourself, "How does this request for my time, attention, energy, and/or knowledge make me feel? Does it make me feel needed? Is there a way I can feel needed by taking care of something for myself?" Taking care of yourself or something for yourself is a great way to stay in Woman Energy.

2. Is this the first time this person has asked for this? Yes or No?

If yes, is this relationship important to you? Are you truly interested in helping out? Be honest with yourself. If you are truly interested in helping out, feel free to do so as long as you have the time, energy, focus and attention units available to assist. Be very mindful that you are assisting, not taking over in this situation.

If the relationship isn't important to you, are you still interested in helping out? Be honest with yourself. You may find that you have absolutely no interest in helping out in this situation and every situation like it. Know that saying no here is deeply honoring to you and to the other person. You are not stuck doing something you don't want to do for someone who doesn't matter to you. This is a great way to stay in Woman Energy.

If this isn't the first time this person has asked you to do this, say no. Unless a young child is asking, you need to let this person figure it out on his or her own. If you continue to say yes to this request, you are simply enabling that person to be irresponsible for his or her life. Requiring people to be responsible for their own lives is a Woman Energy perspective.

3. Would fulfilling this request simply be a distraction for you? Yes or No?

This requires you to have great honesty with yourself. You are so used to being distracted away from your own life that it is easy to say that this is a genuine need that you will be fulfilling. If it is a distraction, say no.

If it is not a distraction, is it something that will enhance your pleasure? If yes, do it. If no, don't do it.

4. Will fulfilling this request or expectation cause you to be depleted? If yes, say no to the request or expectation. Women in Woman Energy do not allow themselves to become depleted. If it won't cause you to become depleted, do you have any interest in doing this? If yes, tell the person that you will need a day to think about it and you will get back to them. If you still feel interested in doing it a day from now, feel free to say yes. If you won't feel depleted from doing this but you have no interest in doing it, say no. Enough said.

5. Will the request or expectation cause you to drop into force energy to get it done? If so, then definitely say no. Force energy drops you into adrenaline which will cause you to feel depleted, defeated and bitchy. This would take you out of Woman Energy.

If you can fulfill the request without dropping into force energy, are you interested in doing it? If yes, tell the person that you will need a day to think about it and you will get back to them. If you still feel interested in doing it a day from now, feel free to say yes. If you won't drop into force energy from doing this but you have no interest in doing it, say no. Nothing more is required.

6. Is this an opportunity for you to grow? If yes, feel free to say yes as long as it won't deplete you or cause you to drop into force energy. If it isn't an opportunity for you to grow, say no. You require opportunities to grow in your own life. If this situation doesn't allow for that, it isn't benefitting you. Either of these answers will keep you in Woman Energy.

7. Will it require you to organize something? Is this your comfort zone? Say no. This is simply a distraction.

8. Will it give you the opportunity to do something totally differently and in more flow than you would have done in the past? If so, feel free to say yes to this if you have the time, the energy, the interest, it won't deplete you and you won't drop back into force energy. If you can meet all of these requirements, you will stay in Woman Energy. If you can't meet all of these requirements, say no. This too, will keep you in Woman Energy.

9. You may not have even received a request but are thinking, "I could do this for this person". Or, "This person could really benefit if I did _____ for him or her." STOP. This is what you are moving away from. The minute you realize that you are having these thoughts, stop yourself. Understand that you are about to jump out of Woman Energy and back into Mother Energy – Intrusive. There is nothing here that requires your input. Period. End of story.

Pay attention to what comes up for you as you ask these questions. Attention precedes a shift. Did you have thoughts like, "If I don't do it no one will. Focusing on my own life is selfish. I am the only one who can do it properly. People won't need me if I say no. My need to be needed will go unfulfilled if I say no. I don't have time to focus on my own life. I am too busy for that." These are all subconscious programs that keep you stuck and from focusing on moving your own life forward. These programs also allow you to avoid facing your fears that maybe your desires aren't important enough to pursue or that you really aren't capable of achieving your own dreams and desires. These programs can be changed so that you are able to focus on your own life and your own dreams.

When you start to be in Woman Energy and move out of Mother Energy - Intrusive, some people in your life will celebrate the change and feel relieved that you aren't trying to live their life for them. Other people will suddenly feel you don't care about them anymore. Even though they resented the intrusion that your way of being was in their life, they will feel that your lack of questioning and do-it-my-way approach to the relationship means you suddenly don't care about them. These people will make comments like "You don't seem to care anymore. You don't seem interested in what's going on in my life." Be okay with this.

If you are in Daughter Energy - whether Entitled, or Self-Abusive - you might be wondering why you would want to move into Woman Energy since everyone does everything for you and takes care of all of your demands.

The reason you would want to move into Woman Energy is because, although everything is done for you, you have no sense of empowerment or mastery. Sometimes you don't even know if you can do things for yourself. This doesn't build up your sense of self. This does nothing to build your self-esteem. Women who can do things for themselves feel powerful within.

They have a sense of accomplishment. There is great joy in mastery. Your soul is seeking mastery. Part of the reason you demand others take care of your responsibilities is because you don't believe you can do this for yourself. Stepping into Woman Energy is very empowering. Being responsible for your own purse is deeply fulfilling. There are very few situations that wouldn't benefit you to say yes. Some questions to ask yourself to help you be in Woman Energy are:

1. Does this request or expectation or interaction or experience feel good to you? If yes, say yes to it. If

no, say no. No further explanation is required. Because of your need to be taken care of, as a women in Daughter Energy you may have experienced and put up with abuse in the past. This question will help you establish boundaries around this and help you move into Woman Energy.

2. Is this an opportunity for you to grow? If so, jump on it. Give yourself permission to try and fail. If it isn't an opportunity to grow, would saying yes benefit someone else and therefore your own soul? If yes, then say yes. Part of your opportunity to grow comes from helping others.

3. Will this request or expectation or interaction or experience give you an opportunity to learn how to organize something? If so, then say yes. Having an opportunity to learn how to organize something is deeply valuable and this will enhance your self-esteem. A number of women in Daughter Energy secretly idolize women in Mother Energy because they are highly effective organizers. Women in Woman Energy are effective organizers. This is a masculine energy activity. It gives structure to the flow of energy. Woman in Woman Energy are balanced in their feminine and masculine energies.

4. Will this situation help you develop mastery? As long as the situation feels good to you, it is likely that most requests or expectations or interactions or experiences will help you develop mastery. Women in Woman Energy develop mastery.

5. Is it something that will enhance your pleasure? If yes, do it. If no, don't do it.

6. Perhaps you aren't being faced with a request, partly because everyone knows you have rarely helped out in the past. See if you can find an opportunity to assist someone. Can you volunteer somewhere? Choose a focus that you are passionate about and follow through. Don't volunteer and then expect someone else to do your work. Honor yourself and follow through. You will feel really good about yourself. This will help you move into Woman Energy.

Pay attention to what comes forward for you as you ask these questions. Attention precedes a shift. Did you have thoughts like, "I can't do this. What will people think of me if I fail? I need others to do it for me. People will finally know that I really can't take care of myself." These are part of your subconscious programming that can be changed and they need to be changed in order for you to move successfully into Woman Energy. You need to know and believe that you are capable of taking care of your needs and desires and that you have the right to do so.

If you are currently living in Daughter Energy, whether Entitled or Self-Abusive, and you are moving toward Woman Energy, you will find the women in your life who are in Mother Energy - Intrusive become concerned that you no longer need them. As you start to discover your own power and your own capabilities, the Mother Energy - Intrusive women are going to push back. Their need to be needed is feeling threatened. Don't let that stop you from stepping into your power. As you start to take care of your own needs and see your potential, you will start to feel alive in a way that you haven't before. Don't worry about the people around you. Most of the people in your life are tired of your demands and tired of carrying you. They will be excited that you are becoming self-reliant. Don't worry about the women in your life who are in intrusive Mother Energy. Let them know that you still care about them, if that is your truth, and let them know that you stepping into your power is about you and not about them. Stay the course. Continue to feel your newly awakened power. Continue to move toward your true security.

Ultimately, the long and short of boundaries is simply this – you are establishing limits on what you are willing to tolerate in your life – the behaviors, requests, people, experiences, activities – and you express what these limits are. You are owning your thoughts, feelings, reactions, desires, dreams, and your truth. You consciously infuse into your day and your life that which pleases you all the while reducing or eliminating from your life those people, interactions, activities, and experiences that have taken away your pleasure. As you move into Woman Energy and out of Mother Energy or Daughter Energy, this new-found essence is the container of everything that increases your sense of power within and you become truly secure because you can fully take care of your own needs while receiving support as required for you to thrive.

17

Changing Your Subconscious Programming

As I mentioned at the beginning of the last chapter, on one hand stepping into Woman Energy is simple. We simply are that energy if we choose to be. On the other hand, we have lots of energy blocking us from becoming that. Our early life programming tells us this is how things are, no questions asked and this is how things will be, no questions asked. We also have lots of trapped emotions that are holding us back from making changes.

From birth to about the age of 7, the mind records everything that has happened without having any discernment around what is being recorded. This means all of this becomes your subconscious programming. Everything your parents and other influential people believed, taught you and under-stood about the world became your beliefs, teachings and understandings of the world. This means all of your beliefs are someone else's beliefs and they become your "Because I said so" view of the world. As you go out to experience the world, everything you encounter – beliefs, values, interpretations, etc., gets compared to what your subconscious mind has stored as your programming. Everything that isn't a match gets rejected.

The purpose of your subconscious mind is to keep you safe. Your original programming, whether good or bad, is the benchmark for all new information to be compared with. This is why it is so hard to change beliefs and patterns of behavior because if they are different from what is programmed in you, they get rejected.

In addition to new information being rejected, the programmed information contains meanings that we have given to events. Nothing that happens to us has meaning until we give it meaning. That doesn't imply that what happened to you doesn't matter. It is just that it has no meaning until we give it meaning. Unfortunately, the meanings we generally apply to our experiences are negative interpretations of ourselves based on our subconscious programming.

For example, when something negative or unfortunate happened to you when you were young, your automatic interpretation was that it happened because you were stupid or that you deserved to have something bad happen to you or that you somehow caused this bad experience and it was all your fault. This became part of your subconscious programming.

The problem now is that in addition to having incorrect meanings given to negative experiences, all of these negative experiences and consequent meanings create a charge on the surface of all of your cells. This charge is always activated. What this means is this negative experience is always "turned on" in your cells and creates cellular memory. We have cellular memories on cells throughout our entire bodies and these cellular memories are always impacting us until they are released.

Not only are these experiences "awake", even if you have no recollection of them happening, they continually attract other like experiences. A basic principle of physics is that "like attracts like". Everything in the universe is energy. Your thoughts are energy. Your beliefs are energy. Your emotions are energy. Your body is made up of energy. Your cellular memories are energy. All energy vibrates and different things vibrate at different frequencies.

Your happy thoughts, beliefs, emotions, and memories vibrate at a different and higher vibration than your unhappy thoughts, beliefs, emotions, and memories. We act like radio stations broadcasting out vibrations all of the time. Everything in the universe is tuning in to our vibrations as we are tuning in to everyone else's. If we feel a lot of lower vibrating emotions like jealousy, entitlement and apathy we are broadcasting out these vibrations. And, we will receive back these vibrations. So, we experience events that make us feel jealous, entitled, apathetic and the like.

To make things even more complicated, in addition to our original programming, incorrect meanings and charged cellular memories, we have emotions trapped in our bodies that constantly make it difficult for us to make changes. Emotions are really just different chemicals that are released by our organs and glands. Our cells interpret these chemicals as particular emotions. As we go through our day, our bodies are designed to process these chemicals fully and completely as we have different experiences. This happens all the time throughout our bodies. We experience something - it could be a thought, a memory, an experience right in front of us, etc. - chemicals are released, we interpret them as a particular emotion, the chemicals are fully processed and we move on.

However, not all emotions, or more accurately the chemicals that make up those emotions, are processed fully and we end up with trapped emotions. Any time our fight or flight response is activated, negative emotions have the potential to become trapped. These unseen energies are like the wind. You can't see wind but you can definitely feel wind. And, just like wind can be destructive, so too can trapped emotions. Trapped emotions can cause a lot of suffering, physically as well as mentally, emotionally and psychologically. Trapped emotions are a significant contributor to self-sabotage and they can make it impossible for you to make behavioral changes.

Even though it seems a lot that has to be changed – negative subconscious programming, incorrect meanings, charged cellular memories and trapped emotions - in order for your thinking, feeling and behaving to change, changing all of this is really quite simple. Because all of the above are energy at their core (remember, everything is energy) they can all be changed simply at the energy level. You can even use your subconscious mind to provide you with the information about what needs to be changed. In addition to your subconscious mind being programmed with a whole lot of negative information, it has a complete recording of *everything*. The subconscious mind works like a computer. It stores vast amounts of information. Your subconscious has information stored on everything you have ever done, every detail you have experienced, every face you have seen, every smell you have smelled, every sensation you have experienced, etc. Your subconscious mind has also archived every virus, bacteria, and fungi that has ever invaded your body. It has a record of all of your injuries as well as all of your thoughts and feelings. It even has a record of the history of every cell in your body.

Your subconscious mind is also aware of any trapped emotions that may be in your body. It knows exactly what effect all of this negative programming, incorrect meanings, charged cellular memories and trapped emotions are having on your physical, mental and emotional well-being.

You can access your subconscious mind quite easily. You can retrieve information from your body using muscle testing. Muscle testing is a process whereby you use the electrical circuitry of your body to determine whether you are strong to something or weak to something. Whatever we are strong to keeps our circuitry strong and our muscles strong. Whatever we are weak to weakens our circuitry and our muscles. You can use this strong-weak response system to ask questions of and receive answers from your subconscious mind.

For this to work, you need to ask straightforward questions that cover one issue at a time. If you ask a question that has more than one answer, you won't get a useful answer, because it is really asking more than one question. Your subconscious mind can only give you one answer to one question at a time. As well, you must be focused on this one issue and not allow your mind to wander when you are asking the questions. An example of a suitable question is "Do I have a trapped emotion?" This allows for a yes or no answer. You will receive the answer through your muscles or your whole body. The simplest way to receive answers is through using your whole body with the sway test. To do this, stand up and allow yourself to focus on the question you are asking. Remember not to let your mind wander. When you make a statement or ask a question that is positive, true and/or congruent with who you are, your body will sway forward because the body moves toward that which is true, positive and/or congruent. If you make a statement or ask a question that is untrue, negative and/or incongruent with who you are, your body will sway backward because the body moves away from that which is untrue, negative and/or incongruent.

To demonstrate this, stand up and state, "My name is _your name_." You will sway forward because this is true, positive, and/or congruent for you. This statement keeps your electrical circuitry strong and causes you to sway forward. Now return to center and focus on the statement, "Hitler was a good man." You will sway backward because this is an untrue, negative and/or incongruent statement for you. This statement weakens your circuitry and therefore causes you to sway backwards and away from the statement.

To determine what emotions you have trapped, use Dr. Bradley Nelson's _The Emotion Code™_ book and _The Emotion Code Chart™_ of emotions contained in the book. Dr. Nelson created The Emotion Code healing system, which is a simple and elegant system for easily releasing trapped emotions from the body. Essentially The Emotion Code process is as follows:

1. Identify the trapped emotion using the sway test and The Emotion Code Chart. To identify the trapped emotion ask, "Do I have a trapped emotion?" Allow your body to sway forward if it is a yes response or sway backward if it is a no response.

2. Now look at The Emotion Code Chart of emotions to determine which emotion is trapped. Dr. Nelson identified 60 different negative emotions that essentially cover all of the emotions we experience. He divided these 60 emotions into two columns – Column A and Column B. Ask the question, "Is the trapped emotion in Column A?" Allow your body to sway either forward (yes) or backward (no). If you sway forward, then the trapped emotion you are seeking to identify is in Column A. If you swayed backward, this means that the trapped emotion is not in Column A. As a confirmation ask," Is the trapped emotion in Column B?" You should sway forward to answer yes.

3. Now determine which row the trapped emotion is in. The Emotion Code Chart has six rows in each column. To make it simple divide the rows into odd and even. Ask, "Is the trapped emotion in an odd row?" Allow your body to sway forward (yes) or backward (no). If the answer was no as a confirmation, ask, "Is the trapped emotion in an even row?"

4. If you determined that your trapped emotion is in an odd row, determine which row it is in by asking, "Is it in Row 1?" Allow your body to respond by swaying forward (yes) or backward (no). If it isn't in Row 1, ask, "Is it in Row 3?" Allow your body to respond by swaying forward (yes) or backward (no). If it isn't in Row 3, ask, "Is it in Row 5?"

5. If you determined that your trapped emotion is in an even row, determine which row it is in by asking, "Is it in Row 2?" Allow your body to respond by swaying forward (yes) or backward (no). If it isn't in Row 2, ask, "Is it in Row 4?" Allow your body to respond by swaying forward (yes) or backward (no). If it isn't in Row 4, ask, "Is it in Row 6?"

6. Now that you have determined which row your trapped emotion is in, you need to identify which emotion is trapped. Start with the first emotion listed in that Column and Row and ask, "Is it _____?" If it is, then you will release it. If it isn't, keep asking this question by replacing the previous emotion with the next one on this list for this Column and Row.

7. Now that you have determined which emotion is trapped, you can release it.

The easiest way to release trapped, lower vibrating energy is by adding positive energy to your body. This is similar in theory to noise-canceling headphones. With noise-canceling headphones, you start with a sound frequency (the noise). The headphones add an opposing sound frequency that cancels out the original frequency. You are doing something similar when releasing a trapped emotion.

To release a trapped emotion, once you have identified which one needs to be released, you are going to use magnetic energy. Magnetic energy is powerful energy and a wonderful tool for fixing energy imbalances. We all have a magnetic field that goes beyond what we can see or feel. As I mentioned earlier, we have an electrical circuit running through our bodies. As well, we have electrochemical processes that are constantly occurring in all of our cells. A basic law of physics states that whenever electrical activity is generated a corresponding magnetic field will always occur. So, we are electromagnetic beings. Scientists now know that the electromagnetic field of our hearts extend 8-12 feet from our bodies in all directions. Scientists also know that when the human magnetic field is exposed to another magnetic field, surprising things happen. Trapped emotions can be released and negative thinking can be changed.

You need to start with the intention to release the trapped emotion. Magnetic energy magnifies the power of your intention to do the work. Magnetic energy can powerfully enhance the energy of your intention to release the trapped emotion and bring that positive energy into the energy field of your body.

The acupuncture system of meridians provides the perfect gateway to input the intention energy into your body to release the trapped emotion. Scientists now understand that meridians are small rivers of energy that flow just beneath the skin. They follow very precise tracks over the surface of the body and do not vary from person to person. Key meridians connect with and supply energy to all other meridians.

The most important of these key meridians is the Governing Meridian. The Governing Meridian begins at the center of the upper lip and runs up over the head all the way down the center of the spine, ending at the tailbone.

Releasing the tapped emotion you identified above.

Since your body is a magnetic field, you will use the magnetic energy in your fingers to release the trapped emotion. Use your index and middle fingers as your magnet. While holding the intention in your mind to release the trapped emotion that you have found, pass your two fingers over the Governing Meridian, which as mentioned above starts in the middle of your upper lip, goes over the midline of your head and all the way down your spine to your tailbone. You don't need to run your fingers that far in order to release the trapped emotion. You simply need to run your fingers from the beginning of your forehead to the base of your neck. That is sufficient. Your magnified intention to release the trapped emotion enters into the Governing Meridian and from there this thought energy flows quickly into all other meridians and areas of your body. This sudden influx of intention energy to release the trapped emotion has the effect of releasing the trapped emotion permanently. You need to run your two fingers over your Governing Meridian for the distance mentioned above for three swipes. Once you release a trapped emotion it is gone for good.

You can continue asking if you have a trapped emotion and determining which emotion is trapped and ready to release. When you have identified which emotion is trapped, it is a good idea to also ask, "Is there anything more about this emotion that I need to know?" Often, the subconscious mind wants information about this trapped emotion brought forward so that you can have greater understanding of why this emotion became trapped. If the answer to this question was no then simply do three swipes down your Governing Meridian with your two fingers to release this trapped emotion.

If the answer to this question was yes then you can ask at what age this emotion got trapped. Word your question something like this, "Did this emotion get trapped in the first half of my life?" If yes, ask, "Was this at birth?" If the answer was yes, ask if you need any more information. If the answer is no then swipe three times over your Governing Meridian with your two fingers. If it wasn't at birth, ask, "Did this emotion get trapped from birth to age 10?" If yes, narrow down the age. If not, ask, "Did this emotion get trapped from age 10 to age 20?" Keep going until you identify the age at which this emotion got trapped. Once you have identified the age ask, "Do I need more information before I can release this trapped emotion?" If the answer is no simply swipe down your Governing Meridian three times with your two fingers to release this trapped emotion.

If you need more information, ask. "Were other people involved?" If yes, allow yourself to receive the answer. Often a person's name will pop into your head. If you still require more information, allow the question that you need to ask to come to you. In general, you won't need a lot of information before releasing the trapped emotion. Dr. Nelson explains all of this more fully in his book *The Emotion Code.*

I started using The Emotion Code process a few years ago on myself and with clients with great success and I continue to use it today. As I began to use it I wondered how it could be used to release the negative thinking that we have and the incorrect meanings that we have given to events and the negative charges we have on our cells. I realized that we could use the same process to swipe these away.

I developed the Magnetic Field Release to release these other negative influences we have going on in our minds and bodies. Releasing the negative programming and the negative charge you have on your cells is similar to running a magnet over the magnetic stripe on your credit card. When you run a magnet over the magnetic stripe you wipe out all of the information that was stored on the stripe. In the case of Magnetic Field Release, you have the intention of releasing the negative thoughts and beliefs that you have stored in your subconscious mind. As you release these, the charge on your cells is deactivated. As well, as you release these negative thoughts and beliefs, what remains is your beautiful, brilliant self, which is connected to your highest self. You really are a brilliant diamond buried under negative programming.

To do a Magnetic Field Release release, identify the negative, limiting thought or belief that you want to release. If you are not sure what to start with, pay attention to all of the negative things you say to yourself. For example, you might walk around saying, "I don't deserve good things in my life." Or, "I am unworthy and unlovable." To release this, hold the intention that you are releasing this negative statement. Run your index and middle fingers over your Governing Meridian starting at the beginning of your forehead and going up over the middle of your head and down to the base of your neck. Do this three times.

Quite often, there are other statements behind or connected to the one you just released. Using the statement that you just released, ask yourself, "How does it feel that _____." So, if your initial statement was "I am unworthy" and you just released that statement, ask yourself, "How does it feel that I am unworthy?" Allow an answer to come to mind. You will now release this answer. For example, if your answer to the question above was, "I don't deserve good in my life," you are now going to swipe three times using your two fingers over your Governing Meridian releasing that statement. Ask again, "How does it feel that I am unworthy?" Allow an answer to come forward and release that answer.

Keep asking the original question, "How does it feel that I am unworthy?" until nothing else comes to mind or you feel neutral about it. Either way, when nothing comes to mind or when you feel neutral about the original statement, know that you have released this negative thinking and neutralized the charge on your cells because of the negative thinking or beliefs.

Another way you can release is by releasing your original statement and then releasing whatever else comes up. Using the example above, once you release the statement "I am unworthy" by having the intention to release this and running your index finger and middle finger three times over your Governing Meridian from the beginning of your forehead, over the midline of your head, to the base of your neck, pay attention to what new thoughts or beliefs are present. Perhaps, for example, you have this thought come to mind "I will always be stupid." You would then release this thought. Keep paying attention to whatever else comes to mind for you. Keep releasing what comes to mind until nothing else comes up or you feel neutral. Once you get to the point that nothing else comes to mind or that you feel neutral, you are done for now.

Be gentle with yourself. You are not trying to change your entire life's negative programming on your first swipe. It is important to know that changes are taking place even if it doesn't seem that way. Some changes become apparent right away. Some changes take longer to notice. Keep in mind that you have had years of negative programming. None of this will be changed with a few swipes. That is a good thing. We aren't set up to handle sweeping changes all at once.

It is a really good idea to rate how you are feeling before you begin releasing something. Rate how intense this thought or negative belief or incorrect meaning is for you before you begin. Use a scale of 1 to 10, with 1 being insignificant and 10 being really intense. Write this down before you begin releasing. When you are done releasing, rate how the original or negative belief or incorrect meaning now feels to you. Doing this is important because the mind has a way of telling you that where you are right now is where you began. So, even though you are changing for the better and are releasing your negative programming and negative cellular charges, your mind wants you to believe that this was actually your starting point. This will make you feel like you aren't making any forward progress and you may feel defeated by this. By rating how you feel before and after you use the Magnetic Field Release, you will have evidence of your changes.

A final note about using the Magnetic Field Release process – make sure you remain hydrated during this work and afterward. The electrical circuitry of your body needs water to function optimally and you need to be hydrated to receive answers properly from the muscle testing. As well, the releasing process uses up water in the body, which may leave you feeling dehydrated afterward.

A woman in Woman Energy understands that in order to thrive, she needs to release both trapped emotions and her negative subconscious programming. She understands that doing this work is part of her internal operating instructions.

SECTION FIVE

Taking Care of Your Self

18

Is it Selfish to Take Care of Your Self?

As women, we often struggle with the issue of taking care of ourselves. When you really think about it, this is an absurd concept. How can taking care of yourself take something away from others?

Isn't it interesting that men never ask whether taking care of themselves is selfish? It is also interesting that a lot of men expect to be taken care of. They definitely don't think that this is selfish. Men simply see this as their right. Some men don't take good care of themselves, but not because they think it is selfish. Some men are simply too lazy or don't think it really matters to do so. A man never stops to wonder if watching "the game" is selfish. Men just simply sit down to watch what they want to watch. Somehow we, as women, have been conditioned to believe that every waking moment of every day needs to be committed to someone or something other than to ourselves. If you don't take care of yourself, you will become someone else's burden.

According to Dr. Daniel Amen, author of *Unleash the Power of the Female Brain*, if you really want to take care of your family, you will take care of yourself first. In his 25 years of running his Amen Clinics, he has found that when women take care of themselves first, everyone in their family has the best opportunity to be healthy as well. He also found that when you don't take care of yourself, it can be truly devastating on both the physical and emotional health of the whole family. According to Dr. Amen, taking care of yourself as a priority makes everyone in your family healthier. Regardless of whether you have a family, Dr. Amen has found that when adult females take better care of themselves, it tends to positively affect those around them, whoever they may be. This is true with your animal companions as well. When you take better care of yourself, your animal companions will be healthier and happier.

Obviously, then, taking care of yourself is not a selfish act, but not taking care of yourself is. It is selfish to not take care of yourself. Not taking care of yourself has dramatic, negative impacts on your family.

Taking care of yourself doesn't mean that you spend all day, every day tending to yourself at the expense of your job and everyone in your inner circle. It means establishing healthy limits on what you do for others and having healthy expectations of what you require others to do for themselves. It means saying no to the activities that drain you and bring you no joy. Taking care of yourself also means that you need to do those things for yourself that you always expect others to do for you. Taking care of yourself means that you take some time for yourself to recharge your batteries and you invest your time in ways that enliven you.

In terms of resources, time is your most precious resource. Time is finite. You only have a certain amount of it while you are here on earth. All other resources – energy, money, attention, focus - can be replenished and replaced. Be very, very protective of your time and invest it in ways that enrich your life. Don't spend it in ways that deplete your life force. When you spend your time with people who don't matter, doing things that deplete you and having experiences that make you resentful and hostile, you aren't taking care of yourself. When you invest your time in people, activities and experiences that matter to you and lift you up, you are taking care of yourself.

My husband and I had a friend, Bill, who was going through a crisis. His wife, who had moved to a different city to lead a youth program, was having an affair with a 17 year-old boy. Bill, understandably, was devastated by this. He used to live in our city but he moved to a city three hours away to be closer to his wife. This was before the affair. Bill's mother still lived in our city so he could stay with her when he came into town. If Bill had a bad day, he would get into his car after work and drive the three hours to our city and just show up at our house.

My husband and I had no boundaries around this. We would drop whatever we were doing or whatever we had planned at the time and invite him in. Bill would stay for hours and then he would drive back home and go to work the next day. He was in town every weekend and he expected us to spend every waking moment with him over the weekend. Bill would follow my husband and me around on the weekends as we did our errands. He sucked up every hour of every weekend for months. He drained all of our energy and all of our joy out of us. My husband and I felt bad for Bill and we felt we didn't have the right to say no to him because he was in such a crisis state and seemed so fragile and overwhelmed.

Bill took full advantage of us. We would set a meet-up time and he would be an hour late every time. We would wait for him to show up all the while fuming at him for his lack of regard for our time. Bill treated us like we didn't matter and he expected us to always be available for him. It was one of the most demanding, draining and resentful experiences of my life.

Bill finally did get his life back on track. He met a new woman and got engaged to her. Unfortunately, they had some serious issues and ended up taking a break from each other. Bill began to show up at our house and we went through the same experience all over again. My husband and I still had no boundaries around this. Eventually, Bill married this woman and we didn't hear from him much after that.

Unfortunately, a few years after he remarried, Bill committed suicide. When my husband and I were at his funeral, we commented to his mother that Bill was always an hour late for our meet-ups. She commented back that she would ask him why he was always late and his answer was, "Oh, it is just Kim and Mark. They can wait." We were the people Bill turned to and relied on to get him through his crisis, and even though we gave up endless hours of our time that we would never, ever get back to be with Bill, he didn't feel we mattered enough to be on time.

I learned a lot about boundaries from this and from having no boundaries with this friend. I will never, ever allow this to happen to me again. Lesson learned – only invest time and gift energy to people who feel you and your time matter. Having this boundary is a beautiful act of self-care.

Does everything on your "to-do" list make you feel more expansive or constricted? Do you have things on your list because your friend or sister or mother or co-worker or church committee member has it on her list and you are simply putting it on your list so you look "as good" as she does? Does your to-do list bring you any sense of pleasure? Are there things on your list that please you? Do you resent everything on your list? Is your to-do list your "wow, look at me and all the things I will get done" list? What would you really love to drop off your list? What stops you from dropping it from your list? Where would saying no allow you a life-changing exhale?

Are you literally going through your day holding your breath? If so, your fight or flight response is constantly activated. Holding your breath signals to your brain that you are in danger. This activates your sympathetic nervous system to kick into high gear, which causes your brain to signal the release of adrenaline and cortisol. The in-breath (inhale) activates the sympathetic nervous system. The sympathetic nervous system is responsible for mobilizing the body during the fight or flight response and aids in control of most of the body's internal organs.

The out-breath (exhale) activates the parasympathetic nervous system. The parasympathetic nervous system is your calming system. It registers safety in your body and allows the "housekeeping" processes such as digestion, elimination, rest and rejuvenation to take place in your body. When we hold our breath, we activate the sympathetic nervous system while the parasympathetic nervous system is "put on hold". This means that our fight or flight response is activated. Prolonged activation of our fight or flight response registers as stress in our bodies.

If you constantly feel stressed or your doctor has told you to decrease your stress levels and you really aren't sure where to start, pay attention to your breath. Always, always, always remember to exhale. Although breathing is an automatic activity in the body, we can interrupt the process when we hold our breath because of stress, overwhelm, panic or any number of negative emotions.

When you start to feel your fight or flight response activate, the following is a great way to stop your stress response before it kicks in. Breathe in for four counts and breathe out for four counts. Do this four times. This will deactivate your fight or flight response. This is great self-care.

Do you keep certain activities going because they are "tradition" and yet they hold no meaning for you? Or, do you do certain seasonal activities because you should or because they evoke happy memories of your spouse's grandmother, but doing so leaves you drained and exhausted? Is there a way that you can do these activities so that you will receive joy from them? If not, stop doing them. If you can do them as a gift for your spouse, you will be in a much lighter, more joyful energy than if you do them from a giving energy.

If there is absolutely no joy in it for you, stop doing these activities. Let your spouse or partner do them for himself/herself. If he or she can't be bothered to put in the time, why should you? This is a beautiful boundary and a beautiful act of self-care.

A woman in Woman Energy understands the importance of self-care and she makes it a priority. She understands that by taking care of herself, she is showing other women the importance of this. She also understands that when she takes care of herself, she is honoring herself and has more energy with which to share her gifts with the world.

19

Powerful Ways to Take Care of Your Self

Most often, women think of self-care as spending the whole day at a spa. Although that might really resonate with you and might do you the world of good, there are lots of powerful ways to take care of yourself that you can incorporate into your every day. Beautiful acts of self-care take into account your physical body and physical environment; your mental space; your emotional space; your psychological space; your psychic space and your spiritual space. Some acts of self-care include more than one of these areas. The most important act of self-care is this:

Stop saying that you don't deserve some time to yourself. Stop telling yourself that you are a bad mother or bad wife or bad friend, or whatever bad person you feel you are if you don't dedicate every minute of every day to others. Men don't do this to themselves. It is abusive.

On the following pages are simple self-care suggestions you can infuse into your daily life. Infuse as many as you feel drawn to into your daily routine. Even adding just one of these will enhance your well-being. All of these suggestions are part of your internal operating instructions. It is up to you to honor yourself enough to infuse these into your daily living.

I recommend that you read through all of them to see which ones initially resonate with you and infuse those into your daily living. Leave the rest for now. As you become ready for additional ways to take care of yourself, the remaining suggestions will already be tucked away in your mind. Your mind will prompt you to read the self-care sections again to see which ones you resonate with at that time.

PHYSICAL Self-Care – The Physical Self-Care category includes anything to do with your physical body and your physical environment.

Shut off your overactive stress response. Your stress response is your fight or flight response and once it is chronically activated it becomes your way of being. The stress response starts in your gut. If it never shuts off, the lining of your intestines becomes inflamed, making it impossible for the stress response to shut off. Healing the inflammation in the lining of your intestines will help you shut off your overactive stress response. A great way to heal this inflammation is by drinking fermented drinks such as Kefir or Kombucha. These drinks are loaded with several different probiotics, beneficial enzymes, B vitamins and Omega-3 fatty acids. All of these help restore the health of your gut in general and your intestines in particular.

> ***Important note about fermented foods and drinks** – If you take prescription antidepressant medications, talk with your health care provider. People taking certain antidepressants need to avoid eating or drinking fermented foods. The combination is deadly.

Eat well. Nourishing yourself (and your family) with foods that feel good to you is a wonderful way to take care of yourself. Pay attention to how food feels in your body. Eat more of what feels good in your body and less of what doesn't.

Stop starving yourself. Starving yourself is such an aggressive act against yourself. This is totally the opposite of self-care. Your body needs an optimal amount of nourishment to be at its peak. Consuming less than that is harming you.

Drink more water. Water is obviously critical for our survival but most people don't drink enough of it. Drinking the purest water you can afford is great self-care. Water is essential for healthy kidneys. As well, all of your cells need to be properly hydrated and the best way to do this is by drinking water with nothing in it. Drinking water is a fabulous way to increase your energy. Our bodies are electrical and run on electrical circuits. Water is required for these circuits to run properly. If you are dehydrated, your circuitry doesn't run efficiently, which makes you feel tired and sluggish and makes it more difficult for you to learn or remember something.

Take care of your liver. Your liver is responsible for over 500 processes in your body. Three key processes are cleaning your blood of toxins; producing bile (which is necessary for digestion) and storing glycogen, which is like backup fuel for your cells. In addition, your liver plays a key role in metabolism and deactivating estrogen at the end of the estrogen cycle. When your liver is unhappy, you may experience, among other things, increased blood pressure, unbalanced hormones and too much estrogen circulating in your body. Keeping your liver happy is a great way to take care of yourself. Limit consumption of alcohol and over-the-counter drugs, especially non-steroidal anti-inflammatory drugs, such as aspirin and ibuprofen. These are quite hard on your liver. There are some great supplements that support liver health including vitamin B6, milk thistle and beet juice. Talk to your health care provider to find the ones that best support your liver.

Focus on your breathing. Obviously, breathing happens automatically. However, as I mentioned earlier, you can interrupt the breathing process when you hold your breath. When you do this, you signal to your brain that you are facing some kind of danger and the brain signals for the release of adrenaline so that you can get the heck out of the way.

There are a couple of breathing techniques that I want to offer here. First, according to Julie Renee Doering, a renowned brain rejuvenation expert, breathing in pink and gold energy will bring rejuvenation and healing to your body. Imagine breathing in pink and gold energy. Allow that breath to flow through your body. Breathe out stress. Do 10 of these breaths to renew and restore your energy. Doering has documented that if you breathed in pink and gold energy for an hour a day, your body would be 10 years younger after a year of doing this. This is great self-care.

The second breathing technique comes from The Institute of HeartMath®. Put either hand over your heart center or the middle of your chest above your breasts. Imagine that you are breathing into your hand as you inhale to the count of four. Then imagine you are breathing out through your hand to the count of four. When you breathe in, imagine you are breathing in ease, love and compassion. Exhale out stress. Do this for two minutes. Breathing in this way brings coherence to your body. Coherence is an optimal state in which the heart, mind and emotions operate in sync and are balanced. Physiologically, this means that the immune system, hormonal and nervous system functions are in a state of energetic coordination. When you are energetically coherent, this increases mental and emotional flexibility and your capacity to be in charge of yourself. A congruent state brings about a sense of peace, calm and order to your body. Do this breathe sequence several times a day, especially after a stressful event. Teach this to your children as well.

Laugh. Laughing is wonderful self-care. It is well-documented that laughing lowers blood pressure; increases vascular blood flow and oxygenation of the blood; gives a workout to the diaphragm and to the abdominal, respiratory, facial, leg and back muscles; reduces certain stress hormones such as cortisol and adrenaline; increases the response of tumor and disease-killing cells such as Gamma-interferon and T-cells; defends against respiratory infections and can reduce the frequency of colds; increases memory and learning; and improves alertness, creativity and memory. Wow, with all of these benefits, why wouldn't you want to laugh all day? Find something funny to laugh at and allow yourself to laugh. If you laugh for 10 minutes, you will feel like you are on top of the world. Even fake laughing will give you the benefits of laughter.

Earthing – Earthing or grounding is simply connecting to Earth's electrical energy. This is a simple way to promote well-being. The earth is a source of subtle energy that contributes to such health benefits as reduced inflammation, lower blood pressure, reduced pain, improved sleep and lower cortisol levels. To Earth, you simply need to have direct skin contact with the ground. You can walk barefoot on grass or have your feet in the ocean, or sit with your bare feet touching grass, sand, gravel or concrete. Asphalt blocks the flow of the earth's electrical energy, as do plastic soles of any kind, such as those found on runners, some dress shoes and flip flops. Earth for 20 minutes a day.

If you live where it is cold in the winter like I do, you can wear leather-soled shoes and all-cotton or all-wool socks while earthing. The electrical energy from the earth will penetrate cotton, wool and leather. In the winter, I wear wool socks with sheepskin slippers while I earth outside. I bundle up, of course, to stay warm. Dr. Mercola, a regular guest on the Dr. Oz Show, is a huge advocate of earthing.

Move your body. I am not talking about exercise here. Exercise has such a negative connotation. As well, it is supposed to be something that is hard and painful and most women push too much when doing it. I am simply talking about moving your body. Movement is such a great stress reliever. Most people kind of understand this concept, but don't really know why.

When you feel stressed, it is because your flight or fight response has been activated. This means that you have adrenaline and cortisol flowing through your body. If you were facing a physical danger, the adrenaline and cortisol in your body would activate the mechanisms required to get you out of the way of the danger. You would literally move out of the way of danger, most likely by running away. This movement uses up the adrenaline and excess cortisol that is flowing in your body.

Unfortunately, most stress is caused by emotional, mental and psychological "dangers" and you don't move your body in order to get away from these dangers. If you did move your body after you experienced these stressors, you would use up the adrenaline and excess cortisol flowing through your body and your body would return to its unstressed state.

In addition to using up adrenaline and excess cortisol, movement causes the release of endorphins, which are feel-good chemicals and pain inhibitors. Endorphins remain in the body for two to three hours after the movement and they bring you into a space of clarity and creativity. This clarity and creativity will stay with you even after the endorphins have dropped back down. So, when you move your body, you use up chemicals that make you feel stressed and you release chemicals that make you feel good and bring you clarity and creativity.

Put on some music that lifts you up and dance to it. Go for a walk outside by yourself and leave your phone off. Skip down the street or in a park. Skipping (not with a rope) is a wonderful way to move. It will really help you feel joyful. If you feel really stressed, run on the spot for 30 seconds. This will use up the adrenaline and excess cortisol and return you to a calmer state.

Important note about exercise: If you are in a state of exhaustion or experiencing adrenal fatigue, doing a heavy workout is very harmful to your body. If you are in these states, you need to be very gentle with your body and with the types of movements that you are doing. You want to do something light like a gentle, easy walk. When you experience adrenal fatigue or exhaustion, pushing yourself is the absolute opposite of self-care. In this case, you need lots of rest and lots of nourishing food, vitamins, minerals, sunshine, grounding and support.

Reduce the amount of alcohol you consume. According to Dr. Amen, author of *Unleash the Power of the Female Brain*, your brain is really harmed by alcohol. Drinking less will make your brain quite happy. Drinking none will make your brain even happier. Reducing your alcohol intake will also make your liver happy. This is really great self-care.

Get more sleep. Sleep is critical to your well-being. If you find that you can't get to bed at a decent time, try going to bed 5 minutes earlier today than you did yesterday. Keep doing this. After 12 days, you will be going to bed an hour earlier than when you started. Do this every night until you reach your optimal bedtime. Then, once you are at your optimal bedtime, guard it with all of your might. Own this time as your sacred time. Make sure you shut off all of your electronic devices an hour before you go to bed, especially computer monitors, tablets and cellphones. The light emitted from these devices interrupts your melatonin production. Melatonin is a hormone that is an important part of sleep.

Ideally, you want to be in bed before 10:00 pm. The reason for this is that 10:00 pm is the natural time for your body to go to sleep. The body works on a natural cycle called the circadian rhythm, which is based on a 24-hour cycle. Your body works best when you follow the natural rhythms of this cycle. If you stay up past 10:00 pm, cortisol is released and you get a "second wind" and you have a much harder time getting to sleep. One of the reasons that we, as women, have such a hard time getting to sleep and staying asleep is that our cortisol levels are reversed. The natural cycle of cortisol is to be at its highest levels between 6:00 am and 8:00 am in order for us to get going in the morning and to be at its lowest levels between 10:00 pm and midnight so that we can go to sleep and stay asleep. Most women's cortisol levels are highest between 10:00 pm and midnight and lowest between 6:00 am and 8:00 am. This means that you can't get to sleep and you can't get out of bed. Changing your cortisol levels and getting more sleep is great self-care.

Regulate your cortisol levels with Wonder Woman. Everyone talks about cortisol as being bad for you. Elevated cortisol levels and incorrect timing of cortisol levels are unhealthy for you. However, cortisol, in and of itself, is necessary for you. Cortisol is an important hormone in the body. It is secreted by the adrenal glands and involved in proper glucose metabolism, regulation of blood pressure, insulin release for blood sugar maintenance, immune function and the inflammatory response.

A great way to regulate cortisol is through postures. Amy Cuddy, a professor of Social Psychology at Harvard Business School, conducted experiments using what she called "power poses". These are poses that men naturally use but are not used often by women. Cuddy found that when women use these poses, cortisol levels go down, which helps the body return to an unstressed state, and testosterone levels go up, which increase feelings of powerfulness.

One of the poses Cuddy tested was the Wonder Woman pose. If you can picture Wonder Woman, you know exactly what this pose is. Wonder Woman would stand with her feet a bit wider than shoulder width apart and have her hands in fists on her hips. Cuddy found that if women stand in this pose for two minutes, cortisol levels go down and testosterone levels go up. Doing this pose for two minutes each day retrains your body to regulate cortisol better. You will feel this.

I have been doing this pose for two minutes every day for the last year or so. I get to sleep faster. I sleep through the night and I wake up more easily in the morning than I did before I started doing this pose. I also feel a general sense of personal power more so now than before I started doing this pose.

The Wonder Woman pose truly is a power pose. It feels intimidating to others when you stand in this position, so if you want people to pay attention to you, like your kids or your husband, stand in this pose. As well, standing in this pose at work before you do a presentation or go in for an interview or face some other stressful situation will help you be calmer and feel more powerful. You can do it in your office or in the washroom or hallway or some other private location.

Just a brief note about testosterone – although we associate testosterone with men and bulky muscles, aggression and their sex drive, women have testosterone as well, just not nearly as much. Doing this pose won't cause you to bulk up or anything like

that, and the increased sense of power isn't an aggressive type of power. It is just more of an increase
in feeling powerful within, instead of feeling powerless within. Doing the Wonder Woman pose for two
minutes every day and regulating your cortisol is
great self-care.

Get up a few minutes earlier in the morning. If
you are going to bed at an optimal time, get up a few
minutes earlier so that you aren't rushing around in
adrenaline first thing in the morning.

Get your children to bed earlier. I read a report
recently that said that children need way more sleep
than what they currently get. Regardless of their
age, children's developing brains need lots of rest,
even more so these days with their brains being
over-stimulated by the electronic devices they are
constantly connected to. Having your children go to
bed earlier will benefit them enormously and give
you some quiet "me time" or couple time.

Do the same thing with your kids as I suggested
above regarding going to bed earlier. Get them to
bed 5 minutes earlier today than yesterday. Keep
going with this until they are going to bed at an
optimal time. If you have always had trouble getting
your children to go to bed, start paying attention to
what your beliefs and expectations are around this.
Do you expect it to be a struggle? Do you believe that
bedtime is a nightmare? Do you expect bedtime to be
peaceful? Your thoughts and beliefs are being broadcast all the time. Your children pick up on these and
your children will play out your expectations and
beliefs. Some people keep their children up at night

for companionship. Your children aren't your companions. Keeping them up at night so that you have company is an enormous burden for your children. If they are teenagers, give them the responsibility for getting to bed at an optimal time and go to bed at a time that works for you. If you go to bed at a time that works for your body's needs, you will be better able to interact with your teenagers the next day.

Have at least one hug a day. Hugging activates the release of oxytocin, which activates the parasympathetic nervous system. As women, we need the parasympathetic nervous system to be "in charge". It helps calm us down and feel safe. The hug needs to last at least 10 seconds. Longer is better. Hug your spouse. Hug your children. Hug your animal companions. If it is simply you at home, hug a friend, a close neighbor or someone you feel comfortable hugging. Even a self-hug will release oxytocin.

Stop crossing one leg over the other at your knees. When you cross one leg over the other at your knees, this indicates to your brain that you are experiencing a threat of some kind. Doing this blocks the information flowing from the vagus nerve. The vagus nerve runs from your brain, down your right shoulder and into your gut, where it breaks off into billions of nerve endings in your lower pelvic region. The vagus nerve activates the parasympathetic nervous system. Crossing your legs at your knees tells your brain that something is wrong and your brain signals for the release of adrenaline. For women, having adrenaline rushing through our bodies in a non-crisis time is the opposite of self-care. If you always feel on edge and you are not sure why, it could be because you cross your legs at your knees. Stop doing this. Crossing your ankles is fine, although it doesn't feel as elegant as crossing your legs at your knees.

Stop sucking in your gut. There is a big difference between having strong abdominal muscles that hold everything in optimally and you sucking in your gut. Sucking in your gut has the same effect on your body as holding your breath. Your brain interprets this as an alarm situation and will trigger the release of adrenaline. Building up your abdominal muscles is beneficial to you, but sucking in your gut is not.

Pay attention to the music you listen to and where. Music is very powerful. It resonates and vibrates. People generally understand the capacity of music to move them, inspire them, and connect them. It can also have the opposite effect. It is important to pay attention to the music you listen to and where. What feeling is the music producing in your body? Is the music you listen to activating the release of adrenaline? If the vibration of the music is activating your adrenaline response does this put you in a fighting mood? Is the background music amping you up? Think about all of the different places where you listen to music and how that music makes you feel. Do you listen to music while making supper and your kids make a fuss in the background? Stop and feel the music. Is it activating your adrenaline response, meaning the music is somehow making you feel unsafe? Are you becoming more agitated? If so, switch your music. Perhaps the music is activating your children's adrenaline response as well.

Do you listen to music at work? Most workplaces are adrenaline factories. Is your music adding to that? Stop and feel the music. You may need to switch to music that calms you down. What about at the gym? Most gyms play music that increases the flow of adrenaline. This is great for men. Adrenaline increases the productivity of a workout for men, but it increases the possibility of adrenal burnout for women. Women need music that is more calming. You will get more out of your workout and you will be calmer if you activate your tend and befriend response by increasing your levels of oxytocin while working out. Do you listen to music as you travel around in your car or on the bus? Are you in a fighting mood by the time you get to your destination? Feel the music. Turn off the music that activates your adrenaline response.

Does the music you listen to make you feel centered, stable and calm? Does it make you feel like you can make decisions easily? Does it make you feel like you can protect your boundaries? Or, is it making you feel angry and agitated, powerless and unfocused? As you start to listen to music that makes you feel better, your body will respond making setting boundaries easier.

Turn off your phone in the evening. This is a beautiful way to give yourself some time and space.

Have your children do household chores. Your children live in your house. They should be required to help with the regular activities that need to be done. Stick with this and stick to your boundary on this. Your children might not be excited to do the work at first but by remaining firm on this, you honor you. You are teaching your children how to become grown up. Your children aren't going to do these activities perfectly the first few times. Be okay with that. You are teaching them responsibility and ultimately mastery. They will feel good about themselves and you won't feel like you are the only one doing any work around the house.

Have your spouse or partner do work around the house. Housework is not just yours to take care of. Requiring your spouse or partner to do work around the house is part of teaching people how to treat you. This is great self-care.

Hire someone to clean your home. If you can afford to have someone come in and clean your home, do it. No one said that you have to be the one to do the housecleaning. This is especially true if you hate cleaning. If you find that you are always resentful and hostile when you have to clean your house, you are much better off hiring this out. This is great self-care for you and you are providing work for someone else.

MENTAL Self-Care – The Mental Self-Care category includes anything to do with your mind and your thought processes. The mind affects the body and the body affects the mind. The mental category includes conscious and subconscious activities including intention, thinking, creativeness, worrying and doubt. Beautiful acts of mental self-care include the following:

Set an intention for your day. Before you get out of bed each day, set an intention for how you desire your day to go. Do you intend to go through your day in the energy of ease? Ease is a physiological sense of well-being. Do you intend to honor your boundaries?

Be present. Being present is a state of balance and a state of awareness. Being present is achieved through eliminating distractions and eliminating emotional baggage. When you are present, you experience things as they are and not as they were or how they could be. Not being present keeps you from enjoying your life.

Thinking is one of the key activities that takes us away from being present. Thinking takes up a lot of attention units and obviously a lot of mental energy. Thinking is a conscious mind activity. When you are thinking and using your conscious mind, all other activities that you might need to do, including paying attention to what is going on, will happen through your subconscious mind. Your subconscious mind is very powerful and can make these other activities happen, but it will be like you are on autopilot. You need to be present to actually be engaged in your life. Being present means that you are not engaged in thinking and that you are "in the here and now". Often, a lot of stress comes from thinking. Being present and in the here and now is much more peaceful. This isn't to say that you never think. Just don't spend your whole day thinking because your day and your life will pass you by without you knowing where it went. Being present is great self-care.

Change your negative, limiting beliefs to beliefs that support your greatness. This has to happen at the subconscious level. All of the negative things you think about yourself and say to yourself are programs that are stored in your subconscious mind. We have over 60,000 thoughts a day and most of them are negative. Most of these thoughts are simply a negative loop that we repeat over and over and over. To start this process, pay attention to what you say to yourself about yourself. Awareness is the first step to changing anything.

Pay attention to your words. Words have energy and words have power. Walking around all day telling yourself that you are stupid or unworthy or that you don't deserve this or that is abusive. A lot of the words that we say to ourselves and out loud are actually programmed into our subconscious mind and need to be changed at that level. However, you can consciously pay attention to what you say and change the words to lift you up.

Even simple things make a big difference. If someone asks you how you are, do you say, "Not bad"? Or, do you say, "Okay"? Both likely mean the same thing but "okay" has a higher vibration to it than "not bad". Using higher vibrating words is great self-care.

Stop multi-tasking. It is an illusion that anyone can multi-task, and if you believe you can, you are simply deluding yourself. The brain is not set up to attend to two tasks at one time. It simply isn't possible. We can only **attend** to one activity at a time. Pay attention to this and see if you can truly pay attention to two activities at the same time. Try to type a document and have a conversation. Or try to listen to what your colleague/child/partner/friend is saying while you are reading a text message. Or try to prepare your budget while you are thinking about what to cook for dinner. Or the next time you are texting and driving, pay attention to how much you are actually aware of what is going on outside your vehicle. It just can't happen.

You will end up either doing one of the activities sufficiently to the exclusion of the other or you will do both very poorly. When you try to multi-task, nothing you do is done well. If you **attend** to one task at a time you will have increased efficiency and will be able to complete tasks to a higher standard. You will feel calmer and less frazzled. This is great self-care.

Stop worrying so much. Sometimes worry is a habit. Sometimes worry is a pattern that we were raised with. Sometimes worry comes from a program that is in your subconscious mind. Most of what you worry about never comes true and it uses up a whole lot of energy. Corrie ten Boom said,

> "Worrying is like carrying tomorrow's load with today's strength. You are carrying two days at once. It is moving into tomorrow ahead of time. Worrying doesn't empty tomorrow of its sorrow, it empties today of its strength."

Think about that the next time you jump into worry.

Pay attention to when you worry and notice whether it is a habit, a pattern that you were raised with or an automatic subconscious activity that you simply fall into. If worry is simply a habit, catch yourself and stop. Don't indulge in this habit. If it is a pattern you were raised with, ask yourself if this is a pattern you want to continue with and if it isn't, find a better pattern. If it is a subconscious program, change it using The Emotion Code and the Magnetic Field Release processes I shared in the last chapter. Worry simply depletes you of tomorrow's strength. Worrying less and having more energy for tomorrow is great self-care.

Change your thinking with, "Hmm, I wonder ...". Instead of asking questions the way you always ask them, start using "Hmm, I wonder why...?" or "Hmm, I wonder how...?" The "Hmm, I wonder" part is really important. When you ask a question this way, you tap into your right brain, which is the creative, intuitive side of your brain. Just ask the question and allow an answer to come forward. You will have a much better answer to whatever question you were asking when you ask it this way. Allow your intuitive side to assist you in your thinking.

Bring awareness to what is holding you back from great health or from living a fulfilled life. Awareness precedes action and awareness precedes a shift. When you bring awareness to cellular issues, such as trapped emotions and negative beliefs, this awareness can drive 99 percent of the release. The remaining 1 percent can be shifted with energy release processes like The Emotion Code and Magnetic Field Release.

EMOTIONAL Self-Care – The Emotional Self-Care category includes anything to do with your emotions and lessening your emotional reaction to life's events.

Lift your mood with Weeeeeeeeeeeee! I was listening to a seminar given by Ellie Drake of Brave-Heart Women and she was speaking about simple ways to feel better emotionally. She mentioned that saying "Weeeeeeeeeeeee" is a great way to lift your mood. She didn't explain how the mechanism worked. She simply said to do it. At the time, I wasn't really interested in this and I thought it was way too simplistic to do any good. Several months went by and I finally decided to give it a try. I'm not sure why it works, but I do know that it is a wonderful way to lift how you are feeling emotionally. Say it out loud at least three times in a row. I find that after saying "Weeeeeeeeeeee" three times, I am smiling. If I say it about 10 times, I start to giggle.

I guess we don't need to understand how everything works in order to enjoy the benefits of something. This is kind of like electricity. I have no idea how it works but I definitely enjoy the benefits of it. Say "Weeeeeeeeeeeee" everyday. I usually say it in the car when I am driving around. I get my husband to say it as well. You can say it anywhere. "Weeeeeeeeeeee" is great self-care.

Empathize with people; don't sympathize with them. Empathy is showing compassion. When someone is going through a challenge, you can show empathy by saying, "I am sorry you are going through this. It must be difficult for you. How are you doing?" This lets the person feel seen and supported. No further action is required unless the person asks for help and you feel good about helping.

Sympathy, on the other hand, is like jumping into the swamp with the person. You want to know all the details. You start to take on the vibration of the person's challenge. You then tell others about this person's challenge. You feel dragged down by it. Sympathy doesn't help you and it doesn't help the other person. It just drags you down.

A woman in Woman Energy shows empathy. A woman in Mother Energy - Intrusive would want to jump in to solve the person's challenge. A woman in Mother Energy - Taken Advantage of would feel overwhelmed that she is going to be required to solve the challenge and a woman deeply ingrained in Daughter Energy, whether Entitled or Self-Abusive, wouldn't even care about this person.

Empathy benefits you by showing compassion, which is always uplifting to your soul and it benefits the other person. This is great self-care.

Release your emotional baggage with emotional release processes. All of this baggage is harming you. You have all kinds of trapped emotions and negative beliefs that are impacting you on a daily basis. Releasing them will free you up in ways you never thought possible. As well, you will release extra weight and you will feel lighter physically, mentally, emotionally, psychologically, psychically and spiritually. Use The Emotion Code and Magnetic Field Release. Both can be learned quickly and easily and both can be self-utilized, as I explained earlier. If you prefer, you can work with a practitioner. If you do no other self-care suggestion besides releasing your trapped emotions and negative thoughts and beliefs, this alone will change your life for the better. This is remarkable self-care.

PSYCHOLOGICAL Self-Care – The Psychological level is the combination of too many negative mental and emotional reactions to life's experiences. Psychological Self-Care is about bringing congruence to the conscious mind and the subconscious mind and behaving in ways that allow for that.

Change your "story" from victim to victor. I have heard it said that if you tell what happened to you to two people, it becomes your "story". Stop telling your victim story and start telling people about the positive things that have happened to you and for you. Not everyone will be interested in hearing about the good, but keep telling it anyway.

Stop judging yourself. Self-judgment is a way to hide out. It is a way to avoid feeling in your body. If you want to feel good physically, mentally and emotionally, you need to feel. You need to feel to heal and self-judgment prevents that. Self-judgment allows you to go into your story. Your story is about your past and it is stored as cellular memories on the surface of your cells all over your body. Judgment of your inner "stuff" is like a drop of glue that keeps your story stuck in place. Are you judging yourself to avoid the sting of the judgments of others? Are you allowing other people to judge you? Once you stop judging your past and simply interact with it on an energy level, the glue begins to dissolve and the energy that was contained in it is liberated. Make a decision to stop judging yourself and to stop allowing other people to have a say in how you live your life. This is great self-care.

Stop resisting what is. Whatever your situation is right now, stop fighting against it. This is what it means to surrender – to stop fighting with your situation. Resisting it keeps you stuck in that situation. Accept your choices. Accept your situation. This doesn't mean that you have given up or that your situation can't change. It just means that you stop pushing against it. The expression, "It is what it is" speaks to that. People often hate this expression because they want to keep resisting what is going on or want it to change right away. Whatever you resist, persists. If you stop resisting, you free up the energy to change it. If you keep resisting it, all of your energy goes into keeping it as it is and your situation won't change.

Stop telling yourself that you are ugly or hideous. This behavior is abusive to you. If you don't feel you can tell yourself that you are beautiful, at least stop telling yourself that you are not.

Allow yourself to feel beautiful on the outside and invest the time in yourself to look beautiful. Allowing yourself to look and feel like a beautiful woman is deeply caring. This look and feeling is different for every woman. It doesn't have to take hours. It can be as simple as putting on some lipstick. When you like how you look, you feel better and radiate more energy.

Let go of Perfectionism. Most people think that perfectionism is a great quality and that it really shows that you care. In reality, perfectionism is a time-waster. You will never do anything perfectly and aiming for that is unproductive. It is also a way to procrastinate and it makes it difficult to get other important tasks completed. Perfectionism is a persistent loop that allows you to beat up on yourself and ultimately to be cruel to yourself. It is an expectation that is impossible to achieve and it keeps your fight or flight response always activated in your body.

Aiming for perfection at work or in your personal life keeps you in a constant state of panic and activates the feeling that you are never good enough. It is likely that much of this patterning is at the subconscious level for you. Changing these patterns will need to occur at the subconscious level. Doing so is great self-care.

Stop doing your children's homework. This is a wonderful act of self-care. Making your children responsible for getting their homework done is a great way to care for yourself. It is also a great way for them to learn to take care of themselves. If you allow your children to experience the consequences of not doing their homework, they would become more responsible for themselves. They would also develop resiliency as they figure out how to deal with the consequences. Resiliency is a very valuable gift you can give your children. You are not a bad mother for requiring your children to do their own homework assignments.

Hire a babysitter. Having a babysitter gives you the opportunity to get out of the house by yourself or with your spouse or friends. You need this time. You are not a bad mother for leaving your children supervised at home. I am a child of the 60's. My mom started working part-time when I was 6 years old and she went full-time when I was 7. When she was home full-time with me and my two sisters, we had babysitters. We weren't left at home all the time but my mom understood that she was a lot happier when she had some playtime for herself. She literally did have play time. She was involved with a bowling league and she bowled one afternoon a week. She had a weekly Bridge group. She learned to ski. Having a babysitter was socially acceptable then. Now it seems mothers today see themselves and all other mothers as bad or evil if they are without their children even for an afternoon. This is ridiculous. You need some time and space to yourself. This is beautiful self-care.

Say no to one activity this week. You are not a bad person for doing this. You will find this to be quite liberating. Say no to one more activity next week. Especially say no to an activity that makes you really resentful. If you never say yes to people's requests, say yes and follow through. This will touch your heart in ways you never thought were possible. This is great self-care.

PSYCHIC Self-Care – The Psychic level pertains to forces and processes that are beyond our physical and mental awareness and comprehension and that have a real influence on our lives. Psychic Self-Care attends to the extrasensory and extraordinary aspects of non-physical and non-mental perception. Beautiful acts of psychic self-care include the following:

Trust your intuition. Your intuition, or your inner knowing, is your connection to the Divine and the field of all there is. It is the loving voice that warns you of danger and keeps you safe. It is also the voice that guides you towards your soul's desires. It starts out as a whisper. If you listen to your inner knowing at this point, your life will flow forward with ease. If you ignore this whisper, your inner knowing will raise the volume of the message and will bring you people, experiences and situations that will draw your attention to the message. If you continue to ignore the voice, it will come at you like a big truck that is about to run you over.

Beautiful self-care is listening to your inner voice when it is a whisper. If your inner voice tells you to rest, rest. If it tells you to turn at the next corner, follow that guidance. Following your inner voice builds trust with yourself. If your inner voice is harsh or mean or defeating, know that this is not your intuition speaking to you. This is your ego speaking to you. Your ego is full of fear and wants everything to stay the same. Your ego keeps you feeling small and afraid. Your intuition wants the best for you and constantly guides you to become the greatest version of yourself. Becoming the greatest version of yourself is beautiful self-care.

In order to develop your intuition, you need to raise your vibration. Laugh more. Let go of the emotional baggage that keeps you weighed down. Avoid listening to the news. Limit low vibrating forms of entertainment, including playing video games and watching violence on TV. Limit your TV watching in general. As well, staying away from people who always complain is a great way to ensure you are not in a low vibrating environment.

Protect your energy field. *Everything* in the universe is made up of energy and everything has a vibration. There really aren't positive energies and negative energies. It really is a matter of higher vibrating energies and lower vibrating energies. Since everything is made up of energy, this means that energies are moving in, on and around you at all times. Your thoughts are energy. Your emotions are energy. Both your thoughts and emotions constantly move out from you to others and their thoughts and emotions move out from them to you.

In addition, other unseen forces are circulating at all times in all directions – at us, through us, on us – that may or may not be for our greatest good. You want to shield yourself from lower, more harmful energies. You can imagine having an energetic shield up around you to block the lower vibrating energy from entering your energy field. Imagine that this shield is made up of pure, positive, high vibrating energy. Before you get out of bed in the morning, you can say, "Shields up" to make sure you are shielded. You also want to say it when you are about to face a stressful or volatile or harmful situation. This is great self-care.

SPIRITUAL Self-Care – Our spirit is the life force that animates our physical body. Spiritual Self-Care helps us connect to our spirit which is important for our overall health and well-being. Beautiful acts of spiritual self-care include the following:

Allow your inner light to shine. You have unique gifts and talents that the world is waiting for. Sharing these with the world is beautiful self-care. Holding these back from the world is harming you.

Smile at a stranger. You never know what your smile might mean to someone. Your smile might be the one act that stops someone from taking their life. This makes your soul smile.

Ask the checkout person how his or her day is going. Chances are, you are the only person to ask this question of that person all day. Know that you have lifted this person up. This is beautiful self-care for your spirit.

Build trust with yourself. When you do what you say you are going to do, especially for yourself, you build trust with yourself. If you told yourself that you were going to rest, then rest. If you told yourself that you would go for a walk, then go for a walk. If you told yourself that you weren't going to spend money on shopping this week, then don't shop. Building trust with yourself is incredibly important. It helps you feel safe and it helps you believe that you deserve great things in life. This is wonderful self-care.

Infuse pleasure into your day, every day. As I mentioned earlier in the chapter on pleasure, pleasure lifts you up, delights you and makes your life better. Make sure you infuse pleasure into your day, every day. Actually stop and smell the roses. Roses have the highest vibration of all flowers. This vibration will lift you up on all levels. Receive the delight of a beautiful sunset. There is something incredibly wondrous about receiving the energy of a beautiful sunset. Sunset energy actually stimulates your upper four chakras (the heart chakra, the throat chakra, the third eye chakra and the crown chakra), which are energy centers in your body. Your spirit loves this. Walk on grass barefoot. Sip your favorite wine. Infuse into your life whatever lifts your spirit up. Do it daily. This is wonderful self-care.

Compliment one person every day. Of course you can compliment more than one person a day, but start with one to get yourself going. Although it seems this activity would only benefit the person you are complimenting, you receive from this as well. Generally, when we gift compliments the receiving person starts to glow, even if that person can't fully receive the compliment. That glow bounces back to us, making us feel all warm inside as well. This is a great way to lift your spirit.

Pursue your heart's desire(s). Every day do something that moves you toward fulfilling your heart's desire(s). Give this or these desires some energy each day. Imagine what it will be like to receive the desire(s).

Intend to live in the energy of joy. This is our true purpose – to experience joy. This is truly your soul's purpose for being in human form. Always, always, always have the intention to experience joy, even if you only experience it for a few minutes a day in the beginning. If you intend to live in the energy of joy, you will always be moving in that direction. This is wonderful, spiritual self-care.

Express gratitude and appreciation every day. According to Vishen Lakihani of Finer Minds, if you express gratitude and appreciation every day for 30 days, your happiness level will increase by 25 percent. Express gratitude and appreciation for yourself and your body. Express gratitude and appreciation for your spouse and your children, if you have a spouse and/or children. Express gratitude and appreciation for your animal companions, if you have them. Express gratitude and appreciation for your income, even if you hate your job. Having an income beats not having one. Express gratitude and appreciation for your home, your food, your clothes, clean drinking water, sanitation and the sunshine. There are millions of things to be grateful for and appreciative of even if you are going through a crisis or experiencing a hardship. Expressing gratitude and appreciation will fill you up, making everything feel brighter.

Multi-category Self-Care. Some things that you can do to take care of yourself cross categories. Beautiful acts of multi-category self-care include the following:

Clear out your clutter. We tend to think of clutter as a physical issue since it is physical stuff taking up physical space. While that is true, clutter actually impacts you on several levels. There is also a mental aspect to clutter. You think about it. You also have feelings about it. It interferes with your ability to feel good about yourself. You also judge it and yourself for having it. Your clutter is also "talking" to you at all times. It is always saying "Do something with me." As well, your physical environment is a reflection of your vibration. Clutter interferes with your ability to have a higher vibration, so it impacts your psychic space and ultimately your spiritual space. So, cleaning out your clutter will bring self-care to many levels of your being.

When we have a lot of clutter, we often don't know how to start getting rid of it without feeling overwhelmed. The easiest way to de-clutter is to do a bit each day. Start out small. Go through the physical mail you received today and throw into the recycle bin everything that can go in there including envelopes, promotional material, ads and so on. Place any paper bills you still receive beside the electronic device that you use to pay those bills. Get into a regular routine of paying your bills. Set up automatic payments for these if you can.

Open up one drawer. Throw out three items from this drawer that are broken or no longer serve a purpose. If you have items in there that can be recycled or donated and used by someone else, grab two bags and put them in the appropriate bag. You now have a Recycle bag and a Donations bag. Remove three items from this drawer tomorrow and either throw each item out or place it in the Recycle bag or Donations bag and keep doing this each day until the drawer is clean. You may have items left in the drawer or you may have an empty drawer. It is okay to have an empty drawer. It is okay to have space. This will actually help you feel like you have room to breathe. Once you have dealt with the three items each day, close the drawer and walk away. If you feel you can go through the whole drawer without feeling overwhelmed, do so.

At the beginning, spend no more than 10 minutes each day doing this task. You can get a lot done in 10 minutes and you won't feel like this is taking up time you don't have.

Balance your feminine and masculine energies. Women who are always in the go, go, go energy need to bring in some flow and allow life to happen without planning every minute of it. They also need to allow others' lives to flow without their interference of it. Women who are scattered all over the place need to bring in some structure and organization in order for their lives to flow more easily. Women often think that if they bring some stillness into their lives, everything would be much better. Stillness is a masculine energy. If you feel like you are here, there and everywhere, stillness in the form of meditation or simply sitting quietly for a few minutes would be beneficial. This helps pull you together and brings your energy into one place. Organizing something like your wallet or a drawer would help pull you together as well.

Women whose lives are very scheduled and highly organized wouldn't benefit from this stillness. Women in this energy require to let go of the tight grip they have on everything and everyone and have some playtime. Play is a feminine energy. It creates flow. Women in this energy also benefit from some light, easy dancing. Especially beneficial is swaying your hips in a figure eight motion. This brings energy into the creative center in your body, which is located in your lower pelvis. It helps to bring in more flow in your body and releases some of the constricttion that you are feeling.

Limit your time and interaction on Facebook, Instagram, Twitter and other sites. Your activeities on these sites impact all six layers or spaces of your boundaries. You receive or send messages in your physical space on a physical object. By interacting with these sites, you are allowing in an "intrusion" into your physical world.

As well, you have a physiological response with everything you read and everything you say. Every time you receive a text or email or Facebook post and the like, you are receiving a hit of dopamine. Dopamine is the pleasure hormone. You become addicted quite easily to the sound of the "ping" letting you know that you have received some kind of update. You need more pings to stay happy. Quite often, what you read makes you feel somehow unhappy or at risk if the comments aren't favorable. Now you have adrenaline released. You end up on a wild biochemical ride of dopamine and adrenaline. You feel happy, then you feel stressed, then you feel happy then you feel stressed. To make things worse, you quickly become addicted to these chemicals and you need more of them to make you feel the same way as you did with much less.

In addition to all of this, you apply mental energy when you read or respond to the information you receive. Now you are searching for something witty or hurtful to say. This takes up attention units that could be applied more productively in moving your life forward.

As well, you have an emotional response to everything that comes in. You are using up emotional energy and perhaps ending up with trapped emotions from this interaction. Now you have emotional baggage that you are carrying around.

You also have a psychological response to everything that has been received or responded to. As well, a lot of what you receive has psychic energy attached to it, meaning that the sender has sent some kind of unseen energy your way. A lot of this psychic energy is lower vibrating and impacts you negatively, but because it is unseen, you simply feel a darkness or depression that you can't explain. And finally, your interactions with these sites either move you towards your soul's desires or away from them – most likely away from them.

These sites are energy and time robbers. Limiting your interaction with these will help you get back some time, some calmness and possibly some sanity. Limiting you time and interaction on these sites is great self-care.

Limit the amount of video game time for your children and for yourself. Very little good comes from your children (or you) playing video games. I am talking about the violence-based games here, not educational learning games. Studies have shown that continued exposure to video games desensitizes

children (and adults) and diminishes their compassion for others.

As well, according to Dr. Bradley Nelson of Heal-
ers Library, video games are low vibrational forms of
entertainment. This vibration interferes with your
children's (or yours if you play these games) intuit-
tion, which makes it difficult for them (and you) to
receive information in this form. You want your
children (and you) to develop and trust their (your)
intuition. They (you) can't do this if their intuition is
blocked from lower vibrating entertainment.

Dr. Nelson has also noted the music in video
games is often created to a specific beat that desyn-
chronizes the two hemispheres of the brain. This
makes it more difficult for your children (or you) to
learn new information. This desynchronization also
opens them (you) up to hypnotic suggestions that are
not in their (or your) best interest.

Allowing your children to play video games is a lot
like taking them to watch the gladiator death match-
es of the Roman Empire. It is not something that you
would likely do.

In addition to all of this, allowing your children to
play video games makes you, their mom, feel iso-
lated. Unless you really don't want interaction with
your kids, limit or eliminate the amount of video
game time for your children.

Be careful whom you spend time with. Scientists have come to understand that you become the
vibrational average of the five people you spend the
most time with. Do you like the vibration of these
people? Are they living the way you ultimately desire
to live? Are they lifting you up? Are they dragging

you down? Do you feel better when you are around these people? Do you feel worse when you are around them? If these five people are your immediate family members, keep focusing on raising your vibration. The expression "A rising tide lifts all boats" fits here. As you continue to raise your vibration by laughing, clearing out clutter, releasing your trapped emotions, not engaging in low vibrational entertainment, etc., you will be assisting these individuals to lift their vibrations as well. If these five people are not your immediate family members, limit your exposure to them.

Enhance your sensuality. Tara Marino of Elegant Femme defines sensuality as living life awake and engaged, using all of your senses, including taste, touch, sound, smell, sight, intuition and your sense of receiving. Can you imagine what your life would be like if you went through each day asking what it tasted like, looked like, smelled like, sounded like, felt like, as well as what your inner voice shared with you and what you received? Your life would open up in ways that you can't even imagine. This is wonderful self-care.

Stop watching "The News". Nothing good comes from watching the news. You can't change what is going on. If you really need to know about something, you will hear about it somehow. The news crosses all six categories of your well-being. It is a lot like Facebook, Twitter, Instagram and the like except that it is generally a lot more negative. The news is intentionally presented to be negative, to keep you in fear and to control you. It is much easier to control a group of people if they are all in fear. Choosing not to watch the news is really great self-care.

See the beauty in everything around you. Seeing the beauty in the world will do a number of things for you. First, it will lift you out of darkness. I received this suggestion from Tara Marino of Elegant Femme at a time when my husband and I had just experienced a traumatic loss. My world seemed quite dark and without much hope at the time. Tara's suggestion of looking for and appreciating the beauty around me helped me see light when it didn't feel like there was any.

Second, when you notice the beauty around you, you actually receive energy from whatever you are looking at and you stimulate the pleasure centers in your brain, which release dopamine, the pleasure hormone. So, you feel better as well.

Third, in addition to beauty helping you to see light and feel better, having the intention to see and then actually look for the beauty around you requires you to be mindful. When you are mindful, you are present. When you are present, you are in your conscious mind, which is your creative mind. When you are in your conscious, creative mind, you are able to focus on your dreams and desires. As well, when you set an intention and follow through, you build trust with yourself. As you build trust with yourself, you release oxytocin. As you release oxytocin, you feel safe. As you feel safe, you can create your dreams and desires. Seeing the beauty around you activates this delicious, beautiful circle of well-being and provides the space in which to create your dreams and desires. This is fabulous self-care.

Say no to your in-laws' demands. You are not a bad wife for doing this. As a daughter-in-law, you are not meant to be at their beck and call nor are you meant to sacrifice yourself for their happiness. This is great self-care.

REFERENCES

Amen, Daniel M.D. (2013). *Unleash the Power of the Female Brain.* New York, NY: Harmony Books.

Andrus, Crystal (2012). *Mother Energy, Daughter Energy, Woman Energy* seminar. www.swatinstitute.com

Cuddy, Amy (2012, June). Your body language shapes who you are. TEDGlobal 2012. www.ted.com

Doering, Julie Renee (2014, August). Interview with Julie Renee. www.julierenee.com

Drake, Ellie (2013). *Female Success Model* seminar series. www.braveheartwomen.com

Gottfried, Sara, M.D. (2014, April). Interview with Dr. Christiane Northrup. www.saragottfriedmd.com

Hay, Louise L. (1988). *Heal Your Body.* Carlsbad, CA: Hay House Inc.

Lakhiani, Vishen (2012). Finer Minds. www.finerminds.com

Lipton, Bruce, Ph.D. (2014). *The Honeymoon Effect: The Science of Creating Heaven on Earth.* Carlsbad, CA: Hay House Inc.

Loyd, Alexander, N.D., Ph.D., and Johnson, Ben, M.D., D.O., N.M.D. (2006). *The Healing Codes*. Light of Man Ministries.

Marino, Tara (2012). *Power of Sensuality* course. www.elegantfemme.com

McCraty, Rollin, Ph.D. (2012, July 16). *Lower Stress and Build Resilience Naturally* seminar. www.heartmath.org

Mujica-Parodi LR1, Strey HH, Frederick B, Savoy R, Cox D, Botanov Y, Tolkunov D, Rubin D, Weber J. (2009). Chemosensory cues to conspecific emotional stress activate amygdala in humans. PLoS One, 4(7): e6415. doi:10.1371/journal.pone.0006415

Nelson, Bradley, D.C. (2014, September). *Awaken Your Highest Self Training Series*. www.healerslibrary.com

Nelson, Bradley, D.C. (2007). *The Emotion Code*. Mesquite, NV: Wellness Unmasked Publishing.

Osteen, Joel (2014, April). Healthy Families [Television series episode]. *Joel Osteen*. Houston, TX. Joel Osteen Ministries.

Roman, Sanaya (1986). *Living With Joy: Keys to Personal Power & Spiritual Transformation*. Tiburon, CA: HJ Kramer Inc.

Truman, Karol K. (2003). *Feelings Buried Alive Never Die*. Phoenix, AZ: Olympus Distributing.

Index

Additional Title in The Thriving Woman's Guide to™ series:

The Thriving Woman's Guide to Job Interviews: 6 Steps to Your Best Job Interview Ever

Kim Buck, M.B.A.

Most of what happens in an interview is based on the steps women take before they get to the interview. In Section One, Before the Interview, in *The Thriving Woman's Guide to Job Interviews: 6 Steps to Your Best Job Interview Ever,* women are taught how to research the company they are interviewing with so they know how they would add value there. The section also covers all of the elements of appearance, including clothing, jewelry, hair, makeup and fragrance. It shows women how to identify their strengths and weaknesses in a way that helps women have a greater sense of themselves. This section also guides women on how to answer the question, "What do you see yourself doing in 5 years?" so that women clearly understand where they are in their careers and what it will take for them to move forward. Section Two, The Interview, covers all components of an interview including the importance of being on time, how to sit, what to do with your phone and how to breathe. Section Three, After the Interview, explains the simple follow-up process and Section Four, Simple Energy Tips, shares powerful processes women can do before the interview to feel less stressed and more focused.

NOTES

NOTES

44434293R00152

Made in the USA
Middletown, DE
08 May 2019